NO SAFE PLACE
INCEST AND DEFILEMENT IN BOTSWANA

WOMEN AND LAW IN SOUTHERN AFRICA
RESEARCH TRUST (BOTSWANA)

No Safe Place: Incest and Defilement in Botswana

Published by LIGHTBOOKS
a division of
Lentswe La Lesedi (Pty) Ltd
PO Box 2365, Gaborone, Botswana.
Tel: 303994, Fax: 314017, E-mail: publisher@lightbooks.net

First published 2002

ISBN 99912-71-27-9

© Copyright Women and Law in Southern Africa Research Project 2002

All rights reserved. No part of the work contained in this publication may be reproduced, stored in a retrieval system, or transmitted by any means without the prior permission of the publisher and the copyright holders.

Typesetting and design by LENTSWE LA LESEDI (PTY) LTD

Cover design by Paul Melenhorst

Printed by Printing and Publishing Botswana (Pty) Ltd

The way a society treats its children reflects not only its qualities of compassion and protective caring, but also its sense of justice, its commitment to the future and its urge to enhance the human condition for coming generations. This is as indisputably true of the community of nations as it is of nations individually.

Javier Perez de Cuellar, UN Secretary-General, in a message to the International Meeting on the Convention on the Rights of the Child, Lignano, Italy, September 1987. From UNICEF. 'Girls and Boys on Equal Terms'. Background Note No.6. C*onvention on the Rights of the Child. Briefing Kit.* New York: Centre for Human Rights: United Nations.

Contents

Preface .... *vii*
Writers .... *ix*
Acknowledgements .... *xi*

Introduction
1.1 Background 1
1.2 Assumptions 2
1.3 Objectives of the Study 3
1.4 Justification of the Study 4
1.5 Organization of the Study 5

Conceptual and Theoretical Framework
2.1 Definition of Concepts 7
2.2 Theoretical Perspectives 13

Legal Framework Governing Violence in Botswana
3.1 The Constitution of Botswana 19
3.2 Customary Law 19
3.3 The Penal Code 21
3.4 The Children's Act 22

Methodology
4.1 Research Sites 25
4.2 The Research Team 26
4.3 Study Respondents 26
4.4 Data Collection Methods 27
4.5 Strengths and Limitations 32

The Incidence of Incest
5.1 Possible Explanations of Under-reporting 37
5.2 Knowledge and Views about Incest 39
5.3 The Perpetrators and Victims of Incest 46
5.4 Factors Promoting Incest 49

The Incidence of Defilement
6.1 The Extent of Defilement 53

6.2 Knowledge and Views about Defilement 59
6.3 Victims and Perpetrators of Defilement 63
6.4 Places Where Defilement Is Committed 65
6.5 Factors Contributing to Defilement 68

CONSEQUENCES OF INCEST AND DEFILEMENT
7.1 Effects on Children 73
7.2 Effects on Mothers 75
7. 3 Effects on Fathers 77

PROCEDURES FOR HANDLING INCEST AND DEFILEMENT CASES
8.1 Recording Statements 79
8.2 The Medical Report 80
8.3 Manner of Investigation 81
8.4 Arrest and Warrant of Arrest 82
8.5 The Trial Process 83

SUMMARY AND RCOMMENDATIONS
9.1 Summary of Findings 87
9.2. Recommendations 90

Appendix 1: Tables *101*
Appendix 2: Proposed Police Procedures on Family/Domestic Violence *105*
Appendix 3: The Original and Proposed Revised Medical Form B.P.73 .... *109*

Bibliography *117*
Index *121*

Preface

This book, *No Safe Place, Incest and Defilement in Botswana,* captures the findings of the study on incest and defilement. The study has been the most difficult so far conducted by the WLSA Botswana research team in its thirteen years of existence. How do adults openly discuss the occurrences of sexual abuse of children in their society without, at the very least, feeling partly responsible for such heinous crimes? Without feeling that they have allowed and continue to allow such offences to occur by turning a blind eye? Without feeling a sense of shame and irresponsibility? Without admitting that they have failed in protecting their children? The common response from most adult respondents – parents, tribal and community leaders, members of the judiciary, law enforcement officers and social workers – was that both incest and defilement were family matters, offences that were better resolved within and between families, despite the existence of statutory laws addressing such crimes.

The findings of this study reveal that there is 'No Safe Place' to be for many children in Botswana: within the home with biological and step parents, relatives and family friends; in the neighbourhood with friends and neighbours; at school with colleagues and teachers; in church with other churchgoers and leaders; on the streets and at recreational places with friends and strangers. If, and when, the children cry out for help they are sometimes not believed, or they are said to cry wolf, or are told that they brought the suffering upon themselves in one way or the other. Yet, for the most part the criminals are either adult males or males much older than the minor children.

The question is, how can these heinous offences against children be adequately addressed, instead of blaming the victim, or sweeping the rot in our society under the carpet and pretending that such crimes only occur in 'other cultures', or are committed within our society by 'foreigners'?

As is 'the WLSA way' of conducting research, from beginning to end, the study was a collective effort by a multi-disciplinary team of professionals in the fields of law, sociology, social welfare, education and other social sciences. This approach ensures that the situation of women and girl-children, and their relationship to men is looked into in a holistic mannner.

The book provides useful information and knowledge aimed at facilitating: (a) a better understanding of the extent of these offences in Botswana, and (b) raising the level of awareness of the practices, and their impact on victims, family members and society as a whole. Information obtained is also aimed at promoting serious national discussions on, and the implementation of, ways in which to eliminate such offences.

Puseletso E. Kidd
Gaborone, November 2001

THE WRITERS

In addition to participating in research planning, data collection and analysis, the following people worked tirelessly – days, nights, weekends and holidays – transforming raw data into a publishable document.

Puseletso E Kidd is the WLSA Botswana National Coordinator. She holds a B.A. + Concurrent Certificate in Education (Botswana) and M.A. in English Literature (Guelph, Canada). She is a women's rights activist with many years of experience, having worked in Ghana and Botswana with women's community-based organisations and non-governmental organisations using gender and human rights approaches in her work. She has been working with WLSA for the past twelve years.

Chikadzi K Joseph is the WLSA Full Time Research Associate. She is a social worker by profession. She worked for five years as a social welfare officer in the Department of Social and Community Development where she handled a variety of social problems, including those faced by the most affected groups, including women and children.

Gwen N Lesetedi, is a lecturer in the Department of Sociology at the University of Botswana. Her teaching areas include Introductory Sociology, Research Methods and Urbanisation. She has conducted extensive research in the areas of gender, family and health. She started working with WLSA as a part-time research associate in 1994 and has actively participated in all the WLSA studies since then.

Kitso Mosiieman is a producer for Botswana Television, but her career originated in the teaching profession. She is a teacher, counsellor, activist now turned T.V. personality. Kitso's evolving career in the media industry continues to reinforce her role as an agent of change. Her vision is to bring about positive change in certain aspects of life in Botswana, in the southern African region, and further afield in the rest of Africa.

Dr Oagile Key Dingake is a law lecturer at the University of Botswana who is currently on sabbatical with the Motor Vehicle Accident Fund where he is the Deputy Chief Executive Officer. Dr Dingake holds a series of degrees in law, being LL.B. (Botswana), LL.M. (London) and Ph.D. (Cape Town). Dingake is a prolific author who has published books on Administrative and Constitutional Law. He is also a legal practitioner who has served as a judge of the Industrial Court in Botswana. His association with WLSA dates back to 1994, and he has actively participated in three phases of WLSA research.

Chipo Manwa is the WLSA Botswana Programme Officer for the Legal Aid Services, Advocacy and Lobbying Programme. She is a lawyer by profession, called to the bar in November 2000.

ACKNOWLEDGEMENTS

The work that went into the production of this publication, *No Safe Place: Incest and Defilement in Botswana* – the planning, data collection, data analysis and report writing – was a collective effort by many individuals and agencies. Our greatest appreciation goes to the girl children and their families who shared with the researchers the most atrocious experiences of their lives so that the truth be documented and known, and that such crimes are adequately addressed.

WLSA Botswana would like to thank the following persons and agencies for their contribution into the study:

- The Danish International Development Agency (DANIDA) for the financial assistance which made the implementation of this study possible.
- Keneilwe Thona Lekoba, a WLSA part-time research associate who put in a great deal of her time, knowledge and experience into the planning of the study, and data collection and analysis.
- Patricia Palaparthi and Anitha Mathews for their active participation at data analysis workshops.
- Kamogediso Mokongwa-Diswai who helped fill in some of the gaps in the final stages of the study.
- Logong Raditlhokwa, particularly for his contribution to the theoretical perspectives section.
- Dr Athaliah Molokomme for the initial editing of the report.
- Dr M.M. Mulinge for the final editing and restructuring of this publication.
- Margaret Maule for logistical work needed for the implementation of the research.
- The Botswana National Police Service, the government hospital administrations, and the tribal leaders in the areas of our study, for their support and assistance.
- Nikiwe Kaunda, Margaret Katsande, Moneedi Merafhe, Daniel Gaotlhobogwe, Rosinah Mambo, Tumisani Munyadzwe, Master Manake, Nicholas Brill, Maatla Mmereki and Banyana Parsons, who gave WLSA invaluable help during data collection.

INTRODUCTION

1.1 Background

This book presents the findings of Stage 2 of a study focusing on 'Women and the Administration of Justice: Delivery Problems and Constraints'. It focuses on 'gender violence' viewed in terms of crimes committed against women and the girl-child – the offences of incest and defilement. The study follows the successful completion of Stage 1 entitled 'Chasing the Mirage: Women and the Administration of Justice' whose findings were published in 1999. That stage focused on the structures that administer justice and the factors that enhance or limit their ability to provide satisfactory services, particularly to women. The identity of these structures was revealed to the researchers through 'following the footsteps of the woman', so to speak, as the women shared with the researchers the justice they sought when violence had been committed against them. The researchers then followed up on the same structures, using violence against women to demonstrate their accessibility or otherwise to women.

Among other things, the findings of the Stage 1 study revealed that:

☞ Women sought justice from both state and non-state structures with the 'family' being the first port of call;
☞ Amongst the various forms of violence against women, incest and defilement were the least reported to the police and, where reported, they had a much lower rate of being successfully prosecuted compared to other forms of violence;
☞ Women's journey in pursuit of justice takes twists and turns through various structures before any satisfactory solution is reached, if at all.

The metaphors of a maze and a mirage were used to depict the endless journey that women have to take in search of justice. It is a journey which, for the most part, ends where it started, at the family level – without satisfactory solutions for women. The study revealed that in their determination to protect the family name, the victim's family prefer to keep violence against women and children, particularly domestic violence, and especially incest and defilement by family members, a 'private' matter, even at the expense of the wellbeing of the child-victim.

The choice of incest and defilement as the subject for the Stage 2 study was informed by previous Women and the Law in Southern Africa (WLSA) studies, more particularly the WLSA Phase I study on 'Maintenance Laws and Practices' (1990-1991). This study revealed that many female secondary school students aged 15 to 18 years were unable to continue with their studies because of pregnancy. Given that the legal maximum age for defilement is 16 years, it was concluded that in situations where cases of maintenance or seduction were lodged with the courts, the offence of defilement had also been committed. The study also revealed that the men responsible for these pregnancies were much older than the victims, with ages ranging between 21 and 38 years. Consistent with the conclusion drawn here, the past few years have witnessed a significant increase in the number of cases of incest and defilement of children reported in the local newspapers. Some of the perpetrators of such offences have been identified as fathers (both by blood and stepfathers) of girl-children, uncles, teachers, neighbours and other men in the community who may be known or unknown to the children. The finding of the Stage 1 study that incest and defilement were the least reported forms of violence against women and that, where reported, they had a much lower rate of being successfully prosecuted was also instrumental in the selection of the subject matter for the Stage 2 study.

1.2 Assumptions

Three basic assumptions underlie this study. First, that, from a legal position, the high number of teenage pregnancies in Botswana is an indication of the prevalence of defilement. Many of those affected are girls who are below the age of 16 years and thus legally the offence of defilement has been committed. Based on existing data, persons aged between 13 and 19 years make up a significant proportion of the population in Botswana (Central Statistics Office, 1996). This group is highly at risk when it comes to issues of early childbearing and exposure to sexually transmitted diseases including HIV/AIDS. Teenage pregnancy presents a major health concern because it is associated with high morbidity and mortality for both the mother and the child. In addition, it is an indication that teenagers are participating in unprotected sex thereby exposing themselves to HIV/AIDS. Teenage pregnancy also has a substantial limiting effect on the educational opportunities of young mothers, making them economically disadvantaged and most vulnerable to poverty. Cases of baby dumping involving teenage mothers are frequently reported (Central Statistics Office, 1999).

The second assumption underlying this study derives from the WLSA study on maintenance laws and practices (1990-1991). According to the study, for the most part, parents of pregnant girls took matters to the customary courts to seek damages or *tshenyo*. Our assumption is that although customary courts have no jurisdiction to preside over defilement and incest cases, some of the *tshenyo* cases they deal with have underlying defilement and incest issues.

Finally, this study is also grounded on the assumption that there is a significant number of unreported cases of defilement of boys in Botswana. Previous WLSA study findings revealed that defilement was predominantly a male offence. However, during workshops held with various stakeholders in the course of the Stage 1 study, some medical doctors and nurses raised their concern over the increasing number of minor boys they have been attending to with sexually transmitted diseases.

1.3 Objectives of the Study

The broad objective of the study is the promotion of the eradication of violence against women and children in our society. The study profiled two of the most overlooked and under-reported categories of family-based sexual violence, namely incest and defilement. We critically examined the social, cultural, legal and other factors that encourage or perpetuate the practices of incest and defilement. By so doing we hope to provide useful information and knowledge that would not only facilitate a better understanding of the nature and extent of these types of offences in Botswana, but also raise the level of awareness of the practices and their impact. The knowledge obtained through the study should also form the basis for recommendations for policy and law reform in the country, which may provide lessons for other countries.

The specific objectives of the study are to:

- Establish the prevalence of the offences of defilement and incest;
- Ascertain the nature of the relationships between perpetrators and their victims;
- Establish the circumstances under which such offences take place;
- Determine the impact or consequences of the offences;
- Review the decisions of the structures of the justice delivery system, families, and the basis of those decisions;
- Review the enforcement efficacy of the decisions of the justice delivery structures;

☞ Raise awareness of the practices and impact of the offences;
☞ Review the adequacy or otherwise of the legal definitions of the concepts of defilement and incest; and
☞ Make recommendations for policy and law reform.

1.4 Justification of the Study

The primary importance of this study lies with its capacity to generate knowledge in an area where little is formally documented. The findings from Stage 1 of the study revealed that both the offences of incest and defilement are the most under-reported forms of gender violence in the courts of Botswana. Incest is a well-guarded secret, and only in the few cases that have reached the courts does the secret come out in the open. The practice of incest is concealed under the cloak of the sanctity of 'the family' and an attempt to preserve its integrity. The issue caught our attention during the Stage 1 study particularly because of the 'silence' surrounding it, the attempt by some informants to justify the practice as 'the Setswana customary or cultural way' *(Ngwao),* and the delicacy with which 'the family', the state and non-state institutions were handling the issue. Many informants were prepared to discuss their concerns over the issue of incest, but only in vague and theoretical terms. The deliverers of justice shared their experiences regarding the legal constraints they faced in evidence collection in such matters, and bringing perpetrators to justice. They also pointed to the difficulty of providing safety and protection for the victims, particularly when the alleged perpetrator was also the legal guardian and breadwinner.

Also, as indicated earlier, the incidences of incest and defilement are on the rise. In the past two or so years there has been a significant number of reported cases of incest and defilement of both girl- and boy-children in the local newspapers. Some of the perpetrators of such offences have been identified as fathers (both blood and stepfathers), uncles (both maternal and paternal), teachers, neighbours and other men in the community who may or may not have been strangers to the victims. Similar patterns were observed in our Stage 1 study. Needless to say, the Ministry of Education has, on several occasions in the last year, expressed its concern over the high dropout rate of schoolgirls due to teenage pregnancies and child betrothal.

Statistics from the Ministry of Education show the extent of the problem. During the period 1997, a total of 2389 girls dropped out of primary school (Central Statistics Office, 1997). The major reason for dropping out was due to desertion (2176 drop outs) followed by pregnancy (97 drop outs). Although the specified number of drop outs due to pregnancy is relatively low, this is still a cause for worry because it is an indication that girls become sexually active at a very young age. The figures also showed that some of the girls dropped out due to pregnancy as early as Standard 2, and the number increased in the higher standards. Pupils in primary school start at the age of 6 years on average and learning covers a period of seven years.

Amongst secondary students, a total of 2322 girls dropped out of school in 1997 (Central Statistics Office, 1997). Of these girls, 1259 dropped out because of pregnancy. The majority of the girls dropped out in Form 2, and going up to Forms 3, 4 and 5 the number of dropouts due to pregnancy started declining. Secondary school education is at least five years with the average age of students at 16 years.

1.5 Organization of the Study

This book is organised into nine chapters. Chapter one provides the background to the study, its assumptions, objectives and justification of the study. Chapter two places in context the concepts that are relevant to the research topic and discusses theoretical perspectives that informed the study. In Chapter three the legal framework that governs violence in Botswana is presented. Chapter four discusses the research process, methods and techniques of data collection, the strengths and limitations of the study. The findings are presented in Chapters five through seven. While Chapter five focuses on the complexities of incest, Chapter six is devoted to the offence of defilement. Chapter seven examines the consequences of incest and defilement. The prosecution, trial and sentencing procedures are profiled in Chapter eight. The final Chapter presents a summary of the findings and the recommendations of the study.

CONCEPTUAL AND THEORETICAL FRAMEWORK

This chapter has a dual purpose: to place in context the concepts that are relevant to the study; and to provide theoretical perspectives to explain the phenomena of incest and defilement as aspects of gender violence.

2.1 Definition of Concepts

Several terms and concepts are central to this study and are defined and briefly discussed below. These include family, child, gender, violence, gender violence, sexual violence, incest and defilement.

2.1.1 Family

The family is a fundamental and basic unit of society. It is the most important of all social institutions in that it is responsible for carrying out more basic societal functions than any other institution (Goode, 1993). It is in recognition of this that the United Nations General Assembly proclaimed 1994 as the International Year of the Family. The objective was to create greater awareness of the need to rethink strategies to strengthen the family and make it more efficient in its functioning. Despite the positive functions the family is expected to perform for society, we approached this study with the recognition that it is also an important arena within which various forms of child abuse and other forms of gender violence occur.

The existing literature reveals that there is not one universal definition of family (WLSA Botswana, 1992; WLSA Zimbawe, 1997; Murdock, 1949). The term denotes different meaning to different persons, depending on the context and purpose for which it is being used. The definition of the family is also culture- and time-specific and in some cases linked to modes of social organization. People have adopted a number of concepts in the classification of families. Instead of providing substantive definitions of the family, some have simply presented descriptions of the various ways or forms that the family manifests itself rather than substantive definitions (WLSA Zimbabwe, 1997) such as nuclear or extended or as biological or conjugal. Sociologists and anthropologists have variously defined the family as a 'single household' or as a group of persons living together and related by blood and/or marriage (Schaefer and Lamm, 1995).

According to Setswana custom, the family can be defined very broadly to include those persons related by marriage, their collateral relations and ascendants. The Convention on the Rights of the Child (CRC) accommodates this broad definition in Article 5 where it states that:

> States Parties shall respect the responsibilities, rights and duties of parents or, where applicable, the members of the extended family or community as provided by local custom, legal guardians of other persons legally responsible for the child, to provide, in a manner consistent with the evolving capacities of the child, appropriate direction and guidance in the exercise by the child of the rights recognised in the present Convention (United Nations, 1989).

For the purpose of this study it is the broad definition of the family based on Setswana custom and practice that is more realistic. It allows for a more inclusive approach to the study of family violence by bringing on board persons closely related by blood as well as those not related by blood. The former may include child, parent, brother, sister, grandchild, paternal and maternal grandparents, uncle, aunt and first cousin, while the latter may include stepparents and their stepchildren. All these are pertinent to the understanding of family violence in general and incest and defilement in particular.

2.1.2 Child

According to Setswana custom and tradition, everyone is a child because one will always have people older than him/herself. Hence the Setswana saying, *'Ngwana ga a ke a golela motsadi'*, meaning one cannot say he or she is no longer a child *vis-a-vis* his or her parent or elder. The definition of a child is therefore relative. In Setswana, while anyone older than another in the community is considered a parent, a child is anyone younger than the other. This definition of a child is rather arbitrary and therefore unsuitable for purposes of this study. It presents everybody as a potential child depending on circumstances.

According to the Interpretation Act, Section 49, the legal age of majority in Botswana is 21 years. There are, however, various pieces of legislation whose definitions of a child differ to serve the purposes for which each piece of legislation was enacted. Cap 08:01, Section 147 of the Penal Code, for example, stipulates that at the age of 16 years any person has the legal capacity to consent to sexual intercourse. On the other hand, according to the Marriage Act, Cap 29:01, Section 16, a girl can marry, assisted by a guardian, at 14 years and a boy can marry, assisted by a guardian, at 16 years of age. This Act, however, is being amended in the present session of Parliament which started in February 2001. Nonetheless, 'generally speaking, majority is the gateway to full legal capacity and it is conferred upon males and females alike when they reach the age of 21 years. A child may, however, achieve majority earlier, through emancipation or marriage' (Dow, 2000).

Furthermore, the Children's Act (1981), that was formulated to protect the rights and interests of children, provides that a child is any person who is under the age of 18 years. However, within this age group there are different categories of children. For instance, anyone under the age of 7 years is an infant and a person under the age of 14 years is considered a child. Once one has attained the age of 14 years but has not attained the age of 18 years he or she is considered a juvenile. These categories in the Children's Act can be quite confusing as to who is a child, unlike the explicit definition in the Convention on the Rights of the Child (CRC). According to the CRC a child is defined as, 'Every human being below the age of 18 years'. This definition could be used to streamline all the different definitions reflected in the various laws of Botswana because it represents an internationally accepted definition of a child. The Botswana Government, by ratifying the convention, signalled its acceptance of the definition.

2.1.3 Gender

It has become commonly accepted that gender is distinct from sex. Sex refers to 'the biological distinction between males and females, [whilst] gender refers to socially learned behaviour and expectations that distinguish between masculinity and femininity. Whereas biological sex identity is determined by reference to genetic and anatomical characteristics, socially learned gender is an acquired identity' (Spike and Sission Runyan, 1993:5). The major aspect of gender identity is that males are superior to females and, consequently, females are subordinate to males. Masculinity and femininity in this sense are not independent categories but are 'in oppositional relation to each other: more of one is less of the other' (Spike and Sission Runyan, 1993:7). This is the situation in Botswana even as an attempt is being made, legally, to remedy the situation. It is here submitted that, since gender identity is socially learned or acquired, either male or female may learn either identity. Generally, however, through socialization of children, each is put in his (masculine) or her (feminine) place at an early age.

2.1.4 Violence

Violence, or abuse, can be considered as any attempt to control, manipulate or demean another individual using physical, emotional or sexual tactics (Wilson, 1997). Power and control is usually the basis of all abusive relationships (Deltufo, 1995; Wilson, 1997). Although most violence against adult women takes the form of spousal abuse, other adults such as grandparents and other adult members of the extended kin could also be perpetrators or victims of family violence. Violence against the child constitutes what is usually referred to as child abuse.

Definitions of child abuse may vary, but most concur that child abuse occurs whenever a parent or an adult who has the care or custody of a child fails to attend to the child's basic needs or harms the child in any way (BOFWA, 1997; Check, 1989). It can vary from benign neglect and spoiling of a child at one extreme to violent beating and sexual intercourse at the other. The consequences of child abuse may include physical harm (such as external or internal bruises and burns); malnutrition (including dehydration); mental illness of a degree that if not immediately remedied could seriously impair growth and development or result in permanent injury or death; and sexual molestation (Check, 1989).

Violence against women and children in the family can take several forms. These may be physical violence, emotional violence, economic neglect and sexual violence.

2.1.5 Gender Violence

Gender violence can be said to be a direct result of the hierarchical or unequal relations between the learned superiority (masculinity) of males and the learned inferiority (femininity) of females. According to the Beijing Platform for Action, violence against women, which forms part of gender violence, includes the following (Women's Affairs Division, 1996:25):

- violation of human rights during war, murder, rape, sexual slavery, forced pregnancy, forced sterilization, illegal abortion, and female selection of the sex of children before they are born;
- physical, sexual or emotional violence, wife battering, sexual abuse of female children in households, marital rape, female circumcision and violence related to the exploitation of women;
- physical, sexual and emotional abuse within the community, sexual harassment at work and in schools, and forced prostitution;

☞ physical, sexual and emotional abuse accepted and encouraged by the state.

The forms of violence against women as stated above, are in keeping with those included in 'An Addendum to the 1997 Declaration on Gender and Development by SADC Heads of State or Government' (p. 21). According to this, violence against women includes

...physical and sexual violence, as well as economic, psychological and emotional abuse:
a) occurring in the family, in such forms as threats, intimidation, battery, sexual abuse of children, economic deprivation, marital rape, femicide, female genital mutilation, and traditional practices harmful to women;
b) occurring in the community, in such forms as threats, rape, sexual abuse, sexual harassment and intimidation, trafficking in women and children, forced prostitution, violence against women in armed conflict; and that
c) perpetrated or condoned by the agents of the state.

The term 'gender violence' is much broader and not just confined to the domestic sphere. Domestic violence is only one aspect of gender violence, and it is used to describe actions and omissions that occur in various relationships. Narrowly defined, it covers incidences of physical attack such as pushing, pinching, punching, kicking, spitting, burning, throwing boiling water or setting on fire (United Nations, 1993). The result of such physical violence can range from bruising to killing; what may often start out as apparently minor attacks can escalate in intensity and frequency. Other people use the term domestic violence to describe violence against women in the family only, and for others it is a general label to cover any violation where the victim and perpetrator have some personal relationship or have had such relationships in the past (United Nations, 1993). A broader definition of domestic violence views it as any form of controlling or abusive behaviour that occurs in a domestic relationship which causes harm to the health, safety or well-being of the victim. The abuse could be physical, sexual, verbal, psychological (or mental) and economic.

The forms of violation that constitute domestic violence, however, may vary from one society and culture to another. While the victims could be both adults and children, women and children are the most common victims and men are usually the perpetrators. However, there exist other forms of family based violence such as a parent abusing a child and an adult child abusing an elderly parent. Often, the perpetrators are not strangers but family members, acquaintances and intimates to the victims (Dobash and Dobash 1979; Mackinnon, 1987;

Watts *et al.*, 1997). Botswana is no exception in this regard. As in many countries, violence against women involves the abuse of a woman not by strangers but by relatives, husbands and lovers (Tabengwa and Fergus, 1998).

2.1.6 Sexual Violence
Broadly defined, sexual violence (or abuse) is any sexual behaviour meant to control, manipulate, humiliate or demean another person. Sexual violence is common in abusive relationships. This form of abuse can occur both inside and outside the family. Sexual abuse may take different forms such as rape, unwanted touching – especially in an erotic way, exposure of sexual organs and showing magazines revealing naked people or sexual acts to a child. As it affects children, sexual abuse mainly takes place in the family, and is usually committed by someone who knows the child such as a father or stepfather. Girls appear to be the common victims. Sexually abused children suffer from anxiety and depression.

2.1.7 Incest
The term incest has been defined variously. According to the Botswana Penal Code incest is defined as an offence whereby a person 'knowingly has carnal knowledge of another person knowing that person to be his or her grandchild, child, brother, sister or parent' (CAP 08:01 Sec. 147). Compared to other definitions, the Botswana legal definition is narrow. Others have defined it in a broad sense to refer to 'sexual intercourse or cohabitation between blood related family members' (Black, 1979; Spies, 1992). Becker (1994: 176) defines it as 'sexual acts, which may or may not include intercourse, between members of the family other than a husband and wife.' Some therapists and psychologists have defined incest more broadly to include sex between stepparents and children. According to them, sex between any 'caretaker' and the person 'cared for' is incest too. Where it occurs between a young person who does not have a choice about the sexual activity and an adult, it constitutes sexual abuse. On the other hand, where it occurs between two consenting adult family members such as a brother and sister it does not constitute sexual abuse (Spies, 1992).

The most common type of incest is the sexual relationship between a parent and a child. This relationship is a form of child (sexual) abuse because the victim usually interprets the experience as coercive and assaulting; the child is powerless to do anything about it. Children are powerless because parents are stronger physically and children have been socialised to obey parents. For purposes of this study, by incest we are referring to any sexual acts, which may or may not include intercourse, between parent and child or brothers and sisters and between any family members who live closely with one another such as grandparents, aunts and uncles, step-parents, step-siblings, and half-siblings.

Though, unlike defilement, incest has no age limit, the primary focus of this study is girl-children, and not women or boys. This is deliberately so because 'discrimination against women begins in childhood, when social and cultural attitudes conspire to apportion the girl-child less than what the family and the nation would offer her brother... This deeply entrenched preference for males in many societies encourages neglect and exploitation of the girl-child and ultimately lowers the status of women' (UNICEF, n.d.).

2.1.8 Defilement

According to the Botswana Penal Code (Amendment) Act 1998, defilement is defined as an offence whereby one has 'unlawful carnal knowledge of any person under the age of 16 years' (CAP 08:01 Sec. 148). With this type of an offence, consent is not an issue, as the victim is said not to have the legal capacity to consent. The implication here therefore, is that an offence had taken place and the perpetrator ought to face charges, the maximum penalty of which is life imprisonment.

As discussed in section 2.1.2 regarding the definition of a child, various statutes interpret legal capacity differently depending on the purposes for which they were enacted. Under the law of defilement, at the age of 16 years for example, any person is said to have legal capacity to consent to sexual intercourse. For purposes of this study, however, and in line with the arguments presented to support the cut off age of who is a child, the cut off age for defilement is 18 years.

2.2 Theoretical Perspectives

This section provides theoretical tools and a conceptual framework to explain the phenomena of incest and defilement as aspects of gender violence. We also identify and explicate the complex factors that have contributed to the current rise in the incidence of these social problems. We recognise and problematise incest and defilement as aspects of the broader structural issue of gender-based violence. Our theoretical perspectives guide the study, throw light on the issues of incest and defilement, and influence our recommendations for altering existing gender relations that promote sexual abuse and other forms of female disempowerment.

The combination of perspectives utilised for this study is justified by the complexity of the subject matter; incest and defilement do not lend themselves easily to one perspective. A multidisciplinary approach would best illuminate the multi-dimensional nature and character of the subject matter of enquiry. In our view the combination of patriarchy and the power theory, legal pluralism, critical legal studies, and gender and development studies, will best reveal the legal, political, economic and social aspects of the phenomena being studied.

2.2.1 Patriarchy and the Power Theory

Patriarchy refers to a system of domination and control that promotes the rule of men. It expresses and enforces the values, beliefs, stereotyped myths, practices, and tendencies that support the power and interests of men. This is achieved and sustained through the use of the ideological apparatuses that transmit the basic values of a sexist system such as the family, the education system, religious institutions, the media, law making and law enforcement institutions, the economic system, and political institutions. These institutions condition men and women to accept and behave in accordance with the relations of 'ruling' in their society. They are generally accountable to men and they promote the concept or perspective called 'hetero-reality' (Hanmer, 1989:2). That is, women and girls are never perceived as having independent existence. They exist with and for men. This paradigm encourages some men to think and believe that they have the right to dominate and control the lives of women or girls. Hence many such men perceive women as objects for satisfying their sexual desires.

Incest and defilement are forms of oppression experienced by women and girls that stem from the way power relations are structured and expressed in patriarchal institutions. Men who perceive women as sexual objects resist attempts aimed at liberating and empowering women. Even when legislative and programmatic interventions are put in place, the ideological hegemony of sexism creates 'an invisible institutional mechanism' which serves to protect and perpetuate male power. Botswana is no exception. Although the Government has introduced the National Gender Programme Framework, which includes the girl-child as one of the six areas of gender concerns, the state has not, as yet, allocated sufficient resources for the implementation of this programme. In 1981 the Government also enacted the Children's Act to promote child welfare but very little has been done to implement this legislation. More importantly, most of the professionals who are expected to enact policies and legislation lack gender awareness and sensitivity and so their interventions do not alter oppressive gender relations. For instance, there are numerous reports of police officers who still trivialise reports of male violence lodged by women. In some cases the women end up being killed or severely assaulted.

Patriarchal control in society is not enforced by men only. Many women and girls also internalise and consciously and unconsciously support patriarchal values saying they are part of their culture. They don't attempt to question, challenge or change culturally based abuse and oppression. For instance, many non-assertive women are aware that their daughters are involved in incestuous relationships, but remain silent to keep their marriages, or to protect the privacy of their families. The tendency to privatise social problems that take place in a patriarchal family is, perhaps, one of the main ways in which the sexual abuse of females is promoted in Botswana society.

Although the power theory also emphasises the dominant role of men in society, it also underscores the 'ethic/politic' of domination. This means that where power is unevenly distributed, those who have or are perceived to have more power may use their power to dominate and disempower. Although during fieldwork we did not come across cases of incest and defilement committed against males by females, this perspective suggests that females can also subject men and boys to sexual abuse. So it challenges us to balance our approach to understanding gender violence. In addition, it not only sees abuse and oppression as based on gender roles but also recognises that power and powerlessness may be determined by the structural locations that people occupy such as age, class, tribe and race, amongst others.

2.2.2 Legal Pluralism

Legal pluralism refers to the existence of a plurality of laws and legal systems. This plurality comes about as a result of the generation of laws by various sources. These sources range from the state to other sections of civil society, such as families, churches and other social formations. The theory of legal pluralism postulates that the state is not the only source of law, and that there are other sources of law that may be independent of, or even in competition with, the state (WLSA, 1999:28, citing Moore, 1973).

According to Molokomme (1991:10), citing Griffiths (1986), legal pluralism is of two kinds: the strong and the weak. The strong version recognises that various social formations may generate binding legal norms which may be in contradiction to those generated by the state. The weaker version tends to privelege the state law in that it only recognises customary law, or any other law which is not incompatible with state law.

The antithesis of the paradigm of legal pluralism, legal centralism, in essence contends that the state is the source of all laws. Legal centralism emphasises the concept of uniformity of law, which applies to all who fall under the jurisdiction of that particular state (Griffiths, 1986:3). According to the legal centralist perspective, law can be used as a tool to influence social behaviour. This is opposed by Griffiths who argues that the view that law can be used to change social behaviour is misguided, because it makes untenable assumptions that only the state can generate laws, disregarding the law-making capacity of what Moore (1973) calls 'semi-autonomous social fields' (Molokomme, 1991:13).

The legal pluralism perspective, especially its strong version, was considered appropriate for this study because it would allow us to find out the definitions and attitudes of people and non-governmental organizations that deal with the offences of incest and defilement on a regular basis. By so doing, the perspective of the state, or formal laws and structures, is not unnecessarily privileged. Through legal pluralism it would also be possible to learn more about life experiences of both the survivors and the perpetrators of incest and defilement.

2.2.3 Critical Legal Studies Perspective

The critical legal studies perspective argues that law represents the views or wishes of the dominant political force. Consequently, law is the political wishes of the dominant group cast in legal terminology. Critical legal writers tend to be methodologically unorthodox and politically defiant. They challenge conventional understanding of legal practices and in the process disrupt the ordinary modes of legal discourse (Boyle, 1992).

Critical legal scholarship is often said to be a movement that started in the 1970s in the United States of America. It has been depicted in the literature as a successor to such earlier radical intellectual movements of the 1920s and 1930s as the US legal realism school of thought. The similarities between legal realism and critical legal studies include their emphasis on the interplay of external factors or biases such as economic interests in the development of legal doctrine.

The two schools of thought share the view that law is not value free or neutral, that more often than not it serves the interests, real or imagined, of the dominant political group, or that law is a reflection of the sensibilities of those who are ruling at any given historical period. They recognise that legal doctrine and institutions are contingent products in an evolutionary process of social change. The critique of law, its theories and its institutions, is meant to break down the hierarchies of gender, race and class. As earlier indicated, critical legal studies assert that legal reasoning is not only on occasion policy oriented, but is imbued with politics. Critical legal scholars have attempted to show the indeterminacy, incoherence and contradictions contained in legal doctrine.

Critical legal studies is particularly useful because its explanatory capacity allows us to view law as something that can be constructed and demolished to achieve the designed goal. Critical legal studies emancipates the researcher from possible paralysis arising out of misguided assumptions that law is cast in stone and that nothing can be done about it if it is unjust. Insofar as critical legal studies articulates the view that law is not value free, nor separate from politics, this helps us to engage with the political, if we are to change the content of laws. The perspective empowers us to critically engage the law with the view to changing it. The advantage of critical legal studies lies in its powerful critique of traditional legal scholarship for its narrow dogmatism and misleading pretensions of neutrality and fairness.

2.2.4 Gender and Development (GAD)

The virtue of the perspective of gender and development (GAD), especially if it is compared to women in development (WID), is that it does not focus on women *per se* but on gender relations. The WID approach fits women into already existing structures, which by virtue of our society, are patriarchal structures without challenging or changing the structures. On the other hand, the GAD approach views women as active agents and not passive recipients of development. This approach deals with power relations between women and men. It recognises that sexual abuse of women and girl-children is used as a tool of social control in male dominant societies. It enables men to assert their power over women thus maintaining existing gender stratification. In such societies, women, are regarded as sexual and reproductive possessions of men – sexual rights, power and privileges of men are enforced through threat and use of force.

The GAD perspective is holistic in its approach. It closely interrogates the totality of social organization, and economic and political life, in order to understand how society functions. For instance, the GAD perspective does not assume that women are in some way unquestionably right in all forms of behaviour or that men are invariably evil. In terms of this perspective, development is viewed as a complex process involving the interaction of social, economic and political forces. GAD assumes that the political is closely connected to the economic and that, consequently, the first step towards women's advancement is to provide the conditions for men and women to overcome poverty. This perspective, however, appreciates that the poor are not responsible for the conditions that create their poverty. As a result it stresses the importance of welfare programmes, which are viewed as a means and not an end.

GAD also looks to the role of local communities to provide support for women. It further recognises that women are often constrained in participating in development activities because of constraints located at the family level. In addition, this perspective stresses the need for women to organise themselves so that they can increase their political power within the economic system (Visvanathan, 1997: 51–53).

For the purpose of this study, the relevance of the GAD perspective lies in its overall strategic approach and particularly its:

- focus on gender relations instead of women *per se*;
- assumption that women are not in some way, unquestionably right in forms of behaviour;
- holistic approach, which looks at the socioeconomic and political environment under which women exist;
- recognition that the first step in women's advancement is to provide the conditions for men and women to tackle poverty, and that the poor are not responsible for their condition which creates their poverty.

All the above elements are particularly relevant to the study of gender violence within the private and the public spheres, because the issue of gender violence can be best appreciated in the broader socioeconomic, political and legal contexts.

LEGAL FRAMEWORK GOVERNING VIOLENCE IN BOTSWANA

Botswana has a dual legal system in terms of which the general law exists side by side with customary law. Offences relating to incest and defilement are predominantly found in the Penal Code, while the procedure relating to the prosecution of offenders is governed by the Criminal Procedure and Evidence Act. The country, however, has no law, either customary or general, that is specific to gender-based violence or violence against women and children. The provisions in both the Constitution and the Penal Code are couched in general terms. It is important to highlight the relevant provisions of the Constitution that impact on sexual assault and abuse of children, as the Constitution is the supreme law of the land. The Constitution can be used to protect the legal status of all persons, including children, and to challenge any other laws if proven to be inconsistent with it.

3.1 The Constitution of Botswana

The Constitution of Botswana is the supreme law of the land. Any laws, whether general or customary, which are inconsistent with the Constitution are null and void and of no force and effect to the extent of the inconsistency. Arguably, the Bill of Rights, which is contained in the Constitution, is the most important section of the Constitution. It is this section that affords protection to all persons including children against any acts or conduct that violates their human rights, more particularly the right to bodily integrity. Attention should be drawn to the fact that sexual assault and abuse of children, within the family, household or parts of the community, is a direct threat to their life, liberty and security, and therefore a violation of their rights as reflected in the Bill of Rights.

3.2 Customary Law

The term 'customary law' is difficult to define, because it means different things to different people at different times. As Molokomme (1994) points out, there are several meanings that could be attached to the term. She argues that customary law may be categorised in three senses, namely: traditionalist customary law, lawyers' customary law, and the living or contemporary customary law. According to Molokomme traditional customary law refers to the traditional norms, values, habits and other principles which have been associated with the various ethnic groups which now make up Botswana.

Concerning 'lawyers' customary law' Molokomme (citing Wordman, 1998), points out that the term

> is more technical or legal, as it is linked to the settlement of disputes in courts. It is derived from three sources with which the Western-trained lawyer is familiar. The first of these sources is rules decreed by chiefs and other traditional authorities. Secondly, certain rules of customary law developed from the practice of requiring that customary law be proved like any other fact before the colonial courts. The decisions of the colonial courts based on these rules constitute the third source of lawyers' customary law (Molokomme, 1994:349).

Molokomme further indicates that the lawyers' customary law 'version is different from the "traditionalist customary law"' partly because it had gone through the colonial courts which "had their own ideas, based upon Western European notions of procedure, justice and fairness, which they brought to bear upon their interpretation of customary law"' (ibid.). The final category of customary law is what Molokomme refers to as 'the living' or 'contemporary customary law'. This is the customary law that is fluid, flexible and negotiable as it represents the adaptations of people to the socioeconomic changes taking place.

From the three categories of customary law presented above, it is clear that there is no single body of rules generally accepted and applicable to all ethnic groups as customary law. Furthermore, most customary law is unwritten except for the statutory customary law (The Customary Courts Act), and its provisions do not include sexual abuse of any type. Also, available literature does not directly address itself to the issue of how, according to customary law(s), the offence of sexual abuse of children was or is handled in Botswana.

According to Molokomme and Mokobi (1997:186) 'traditional customary law does not treat the rights of children, or of any other group for that matter, separately from those of the family as a unit'. Nonetheless, Ncube (1998:8–9) points out that:

> African culture values the integrity and dignity of children and hence is at one with

the principal values of participation, protection from harm and harmonious rounded growth and development enshrined in the international instruments on children's rights. The philosophy underlying children's rights is as much Western as it is African. The methods and processes to secure the rights of children may vary quite considerably from one culture to another and from region to region…

Furthermore, '…reproduction was ideally permitted only within marriage' (Ncube, 1998: 187) and pre-marital sexual intercourse was frowned upon. According to Roberts and Comaroff (1971:97-123), among the Bakgatla of Botswana 'premarital pregnancy, which is now common and more accepted, was previously considered a disgrace. In the latter half of the nineteenth century, babies born out of wedlock were often put to death'. This indicates that in Botswana premarital sexual intercourse was not permitted.

3.3 The Penal Code

In Botswana, the relevant statute that creates and prescribes punishment of criminal offences such as rape, assault, incest and defilement is predominantly the Penal Code. Thus, a few references to the Penal Code would at this juncture be appropriate. Sections 168 to 169 of the Penal Code create the offence of incest. The Penal Code defines incest as an offence where a person 'knowingly has carnal knowledge of another person knowing that person to be his or her grandchild, child, brother, sister or parent'. Section 170 elaborates on the expressions 'brother' and 'sister' to include half-brother and half-sister. It may be noted that the definition leaves out other blood relations such as uncle, niece, nephew and cousin. It focuses on the nuclear family members.

Section 169 of the Penal Code stipulates that 'Any female person of or above the age of 16 years who with her consent permits her grandfather, father, brother, or son to have carnal knowledge of her (knowing him to be her grandfather, father, brother, or son, as the case may be) is guilty of an offence and is liable to imprisonment for a term not exceeding five years'. Understandably, this section is supposed to complement section 168. However, it fails to address cases involving male persons. In light of section 168, which has since been amended and refers to any person regardless of their gender, Section 169 should similarly be amended to become gender inclusive.

Based on Section 171, no offence under Sections 168 and 169 can be prosecuted without the written consent of the Attorney General.

3.4 The Children's Act

The Children's Act was formulated to protect the rights and interests of the child. Among its main provisions is the protection of children from abuse. It is important for the society to mitigate against the abuse of children because when a person is abused as a child they become damaged psychologically. The tendency is for abused persons to perpetuate the abuse on other helpless people when they become adults, thus creating a vicious cycle of abuse. The provisions of the Children's Act are compliant with Article 19 Section 1 of the Convention on the Rights of the Child (CRC) which deals with protection from abuse and neglect. The section states that:

> States Parties shall take appropriate legislative, administrative, social and educational measures to protect the child from all forms of physical or mental violence, injury or abuse, neglect treatment, maltreatment, or exploitation including sexual abuse, while in the care of parent(s) legal guardian(s) or any other person who has the care of the child (United Nations, 1989).

Such protective measures should, as appropriate, include effective procedures for the establishment of social programs to provide necessary support for the child and for those who have the care of the child, as well as for other forms of prevention and for identification, reporting, referral, investigation, treatment and follow-up of instances of child maltreatment described heretofore, and, as appropriate, for judicial involvement (United Nations, 1989).

According to Section 11 of the Children's Act, ill-treatment and neglect of a child is a criminal offence. For purposes of this section a child is deemed to have been neglected if the parent or guardian or any person having the custody of the child 'exposes the child to conditions or circumstances, which are likely to cause him physical, mental or psychological distress or damage'. Therefore, any parent or guardian of a child or any person having the custody of a child who neglects, ill-treats or exploits the child or allows or causes him to be neglected, ill-treated or exploited shall be guilty of an offence.

Both the CRC and the Children's Act were formulated using the 'best interests of the child' principle. In all actions concerning children, whether undertaken by public or private social welfare institution, courts of law, administrative authorities or legislative bodies, the best interests of the child shall be a primary consideration. States parties shall ensure that the institutions, services and facilities responsible for the care or protection of children shall conform with the standards established by competent authorities, particularly in the areas of safety, health, in the number and suitability of their staff and competent supervision. As a result, children who are subjected to abusive practices can be helped.

The Children's Act, therefore, provides for all children in need of care and protection from such practices. The protection for the rights and freedoms of such a child are enshrined in the Act. However, implementing the Act has been constrained by lack of, or inadequate, structures such as foster homes, children's homes and services that would enable law enforcers to carry out their work and protect children effectively. The effective delivery of services has also been impeded by the lack of human resources, especially social welfare officers compounded by lack of transport and other services (WLSA, 2000). This is an important factor because Botswana is a vast country, and practices of sexual abuse also happen in the remotest areas.

METHODOLOGY

This chapter describes the procedures that were used to collect the information used by the study. It is organised into five sections. Section one presents a description of the research sites or areas from which data was collected. While section two focuses on the research team, section three profiles the groups targeted by the study and the procedures used to select them. Sections four and five present the methods of data collection and the strengths and limitations of the research process, and data collection techniques, respectively.

4.1 Research Sites

The study incorporated a pilot study and the main study. The aim of the pilot study was to test methods and techniques of data collection and the time frame within which data could be successfully collected. The pilot study was conducted in Gaborone city. The choice of Gaborone was to enable all the researchers to be together throughout the pilot study process for the purpose of supporting each other if and when faced with difficulties in the process of data collection in view of the sensitivity of the research topic.

The specific sites for the pilot study were Old Naledi and the Broadhurst areas of Gaborone. Old Naledi is an upgraded squatter area. It is a high density area dominated by poor people, many of whom either have low paying jobs or are unemployed. Broadhurst, on the other hand, is an area comprising people of different socioeconomic backgrounds. This is evident in the types of residential areas which make up the area namely, Self Help Housing Agency (SHAA) housing[1], Botswana Housing Corporation (BHC)[2] 'low', 'medium' and 'high' cost housing, as well as government-allocated plots.

The main study was conducted in greater Gaborone and greater Francistown. The rationale for choosing 'greater' Gaborone and Francistown was to capture some of the surrounding areas as well as the differences between the rural and

---

[1] SHHA is a Government structure set up to provide housing for ownership purposes to low income groups who do not qualify for commercial bank loans.
[2] BHC is a parastatal organisation mandated to provide housing to the general public.

urban. The actual study sites included areas within each of the two cities and selected surrounding villages as follows:

Greater Gaborone	*Greater Francistown*
Old Naledi	Kutlwano
Broadhurst	Tatitown
Gaborone West	Masunga
Mogoditshane	Tonota
Mochudi	Tutume

Gaborone and Francistown are the only two cities in Botswana. The former is located in the south of the country and as the capital city; it is the administrative and policy headquarters of Government. Gaborone is also the headquarters of the Botswana Police Services that deal with issues of incest and defilement on a regular basis. The city of Francistown, on the other hand, is located in the north of the country and serves as the administrative centre for the northern parts of the country. Both Gaborone and Francistown also provide services to their surrounding villages and settlements. The population of the two cities comprises people from the various ethnic groups in the country as well as a large number of non-citizens of various origins.

4.2 The Research Team

The research team comprised full time staff, part time research associates and research assistants made up of lawyers, social scientists, university students and teachers. Due to the busy schedules of most of the regular WLSA part time research associates, it became necessary to seek the assistance of schoolteachers and university students in various fields of study. That notwithstanding, the multidisciplinary nature of the research team proved advantageous in that the lawyers in the group would readily recite the relevant statutory provisions while the social scientists would locate the operation of the law within the lived realities of the perpetrators and victims.

4.3 Study Respondents

The study targeted the categories of respondents below.

☞ Both female and male survivors of incest and defilement. Children and adults alike were to be the primary sources of information. In view of the sensitive nature of the focus of our study and our experiences during the first stage of the study regarding the secrecy surrounding offences of incest and defilement, we anticipated difficulties in getting the information we required. We thus decided that our entry point would be our partner NGOs, particularly those in the human rights network, as well as government agencies with whom we have had a good working relationship.

☞ Significant others – those persons identified by the survivors as having played some role in the matter such as perpetrators, witnesses, family members and others.

☞ Personnel in both governmental and non-governmental structures of justice delivery who deal with such cases. These included the police, magistrates, doctors, tribal leaders and administrators and NGO representatives.

☞ Secondary school students. Participants were drawn from both Community Junior Secondary Schools and Senior Secondary Schools. Community Junior Secondary Schools cater for students from Forms 1 to 3, that is, from the eighth to tenth year of schooling. Generally, their ages range between 13 and 16 years. Senior secondary schools encompass Forms IV and V. These were aged between 16 and 18 years.

4.4 Data Collection Methods

Multiple methods of data collection were employed for the study. These were literature review, law review, examination of records, key-informant interviews, case studies, group discussions, and workshops.

4.4.1 Document Analysis

Data was collected from various documents. These included records from police stations, magistrate courts, customary courts, hospital/clinic antenatal records, clients' records of NGOs dealing with incidences of sexual abuse, and newspaper articles. The police stations and customary and magistrate courts visited are presented in Appendix 1, Table A1.

Police Records
Five police stations in greater Gaborone and five in greater Francistown were

sampled. At every police station, only case records of incest, defilement and 'rape' of girls under the age of 16 were closely examined. Cases of 'rape' were examined because the police often framed a significant number of defilement cases as rape.

Medical Records
Antenatal labour and delivery records were examined for the years between 1994 and 1998 inclusively. The aim was to find out how many of the pregnant mothers were under the age of 16 years as this is the maximum age for defilement. Since it is possible that some of the pregnant girls aged 16 years conceived at age 15, those aged 16 were included in the study. In greater Gaborone two clinics, one in Old Naledi and the other in the Broadhurst area, were visited for this purpose, while in greater Francistown two clinics and one primary hospital were visited.

Customary Court Records
Customary courts in the country do not have jurisdiction to hear cases of incest and defilement. Nonetheless, for purposes of this study, *tshenyo,* or seduction, cases were examined for the period between 1994 and 1999 at selected courts at the research areas. In all, nine customary courts – four in greater Gaborone and five in greater Francistown – were visited during the study (see Appendix 1, Table A1 for the specific customary courts visited in each area). The aim was to select and closely examine only those cases of girls who fell pregnant under the age of 16 years.

Magistrate Court Records
Magistrate court records were examined for cases of incest and defilement. In greater Gaborone, records from the Gaborone West, Broadhurst and Mochudi magistrate courts were utilised. For greater Francistown, on the other hand, records from the Francistown and Masunga Magistrate Courts were examined. The Francistown Magistrate court caters for all the research sites within the city as well as handling cases from Tonota and Tutume. Cases from Tonota and Tutume are heard and the records kept at the court in Francistown. Masunga, however, has a magistrate court structure as well as a court clerk. Although a magistrate was resident in Masunga during Stage 1 of this study, there was none at the time of data collection for this stage. However, cases were heard and records kept at the magistrate court in Masunga by magistrates who commute from Francistown on a regular basis.

Non-Governmental Organizations
Information was collected from Childline Botswana[3] and Metlhaetsile Women's Informtaion Centre[4]. A total of 27 cases of sexual abuse were examined, the majority of which were from Childline.

Newspaper Articles
Articles from the local newspapers were reviewed focusing on their coverage of incest and defilement cases. This was done to evaluate the media's coverage of these cases.

4.4.2 Group Discussions
Group discussions were held with secondary school students, the police and chiefs (or tribal leaders). A total of 260 students, 51 police officers and 53 tribal leaders participated in the discussions. A detailed depiction of the number of participants in each category by gender is presented in Appendix 1, Table A2.

Students
The student participants were drawn from 14 secondary schools, seven each from greater Gaborone and greater Francistown (see Appendix 1, Table A3). During the discussions held with them, the participatory approach using the brainstorming technique was utilised. The researchers decided to adopt the brainstorming technique for two main reasons. Firstly, to break the ice and secondly to jump-start the discussions. The topics of defilement and incest were addressed separately. The approach for either topic, however, was the same as will be shown below. Because of the sensitivity of the practice of incest, the discussions commenced with defilement.

Essentially the brainstorming session was characterised by two steps:

Step 1: What comes to your mind when you hear the words 'defilement' or 'incest'? Here the participants were asked to indicate the first things that came to their minds without trying to rationalise them or thinking them through. Also, they were requested not to wait to be asked to speak but rather just say it out loud.

Step 2: Once everything said – words or phrases – had been recorded on the flip-chart, the participants were asked to define the concepts using what

---

[3] Childline Botswana is an NGO which addresses issues of abuse of children in Botswana.
[4] Metlhaetsile is an NGO which provides legal aid services, including legal education and court reprsentation.

had been recorded or any other words. All the definitions provided were also recorded on flip-charts.

Having completed the brainstorming session the researchers decided to engage the students in debates. The debating was characterised by four stages, as shown below.

Stage 1: The researchers provided the students with the legal definition of the concept as provided in the Penal Code then asked them to compare and contrast their definitions with the legal ones. This was followed by discussions. Where the students asked for definitions of certain terms such as 'carnal knowledge' and 'unlawful', 'child' and 'parent', the questions were thrown back at them. The researchers allowed definitions from everyone who was able to do so and they wrote everything on flip-chart, followed by discussions and clarifications.

Stage 2: The researchers asked the students if they knew what the law provided for with respect to punishment of the offences which the study focused on and sought recommendations as to the form(s) of and appropriate punishment(s) for the offences. Everything was recorded on flip-charts without interruption.

Stage 3: The researchers requested justification of the responses provided by the students. It should be indicated here that students differed on this, and lengthy discussions among themselves were allowed to go on for some time without interruption. The task of the researchers here was to facilitate free-flowing exchanges of ideas. In their justification to each other they gave examples of experiences (without mentioning names) and effects on victims.

Stage 4: The students were provided with the actual punishment provided by our law. This was then followed by discussions.

Police

Discussions were conducted at seven police stations, five in greater Gaborone and two in greater Francistown. For greater Gaborone the participating police stations were Old Naledi, Broadhurst, Gaborone West, Gaborone Central and Mochudi, while for greater Francistown officers in Tatitown and Tonota police stations participated is group discussions. Appendix 1, Table A4 presents the distribution of police officers participating in group discussions by station and sex. In all cases group discussions were held after the examination of the police station's records and were guided by the information collected from such records.

Information from police records was particularly useful in that where they tended to theorise, or explain their responses according to the letter of the law, we challenged them by citing from their own records that were contrary to their theories or the letter of the law.

Tribal Leaders
Discussions were held with tribal leaders focusing on the Penal Code Amendment as it provides for the offences of rape, incest and defilement. The group discussions were held in six areas, two in greater Gaborone and four in greater Francistown. The areas covered in greater Gaborone were Mogoditshane and Mochudi, as well as Gaborone itself, while Masunga, Tutume, Tonota and Francistown itself were covered for greater Francistown. Appendix 1, Table A5 summarises the number of tribal leaders participating in group discussion by area and gender.

The purpose of the discussions held with tribal leaders was to find out the position of Setswana customary law regarding incest and defilement, their definitions, what steps were taken in cases of such acts as well as their knowledge and views regarding the general law position. In the process of collecting data through discussions with tribal leaders, the researchers also disseminated information to participants regarding the position of the general law where their knowledge was found to be lacking.

4.4.3 Workshops

Two workshops – one in Gaborone and the other in Francistown – were conducted with stakeholders from various governmental and non-governmental organizations. Participants included the police, and health and social welfare officers including doctors, teachers, magistrates and state attorneys as well as NGOs (see Appendix 1, Table A6). The workshops focused on the review of two major issues. Those were, police procedures and police medical/sexual assault forms completed by doctors as part of evidence gathering in cases of assault including sexual violence or abuse. The review of police procedures had been proposed by the women's human rights organizations in the country, of which WLSA is an active member. Thus, through the workshops, the research team, in addition to collecting data, was involved in reviewing documents for policy intervention and simultaneously committing the police to the ownership of these documents.

4.4.4 Case Studies

For case studies, the following persons were interviewed:

- a divorced mother of five children who alleged that her husband sexually abused their girl-children (biological) starting when they were seven years of age;
- a girl aged 14 who was sexually abused by her stepfather since she was 11 years old; and
- a mother of a four-year-old girl who was abused by a boy resident in the same neighbourhood.

4.4.5 Interviews with Key Informants

Interviews were also conducted with key informants drawn from NGOs and the government sector. From the non-governmental sector, organizations which address issues of violence against women and children and provide counselling services and court representations, such as Metlhaetsile Women's Information Centre, Kagisano Women's Shelter, Childline and SOS were targeted. Those interviewed from the government sector were mainly drawn from the Attorney General's Chambers, government hospitals and the police. Appendix 1, Table A7 presents a detailed depiction of the key informants by area of study.

4.5 Strengths and Limitations

Two major strengths were identified with the research process and methods of data collection employed by this study. First, these allowed the entire research team to jointly conduct interviews in one area. The advantage of this was that where difficulties were encountered the research team immediately discussed and resolved them, and then continued with the task at hand. For instance, at the start of the pilot study the research team had decided to examine only those police dockets where the offences were classified as incest and defilement. However, at one of the police stations the CID Inspector assigned to assist them by the Station Commander advised them to look at all cases categorised as 'offences against morality'. According to him, some cases may not be reported as defilement or incest and also the police may not charge the accused with such offences. The charge on the police docket would indicate a different offence whereas if and when the case reaches the magistrate court, certain issues may arise pointing to either incest or defilement. The research team heeded the officer's advice and when going through the records they immediately realised that certain cases that fell under the broad classification of 'offences against morality' could easily be set aside. On the basis of this the decision was reached to focus on all cases of a sexual nature. The same approach was used during the main study.

Second, most of the records examined were detailed and highly informative. The police records gave the researchers the distinct advantage of arming them with the necessary information that enabled us to critically engage the police in issues during the group discussions.

The techniques of data collection, however, were not without limitations. To start with, it was not easy to identify survivors of incest and defilement because of the secrecy surrounding the practices. Even where the identities of survivors were known through examination of records, the sensitive nature of the topic made it very difficult to follow up on the cases and interview the survivors. It was also difficult to engage adults on issues of incest. They were idealistic in their discussions. Instead of addressing the problem, they immediately dismissed the practice as not part of the Setswana culture. Finally, owing to some other pressing matters, the entire research team could not be sustained for the duration of the study. This no doubt undermined the efficiency of the team and the diversity of opinions that were available in cases that needed interpretative meanings.

The Incidence of Incest

Incest is one of those categories of offences in Botswana which are under-researched, under-documented, under-reported and in which the offender is rarely punished. This is clearly evident from the findings of this study, which show relatively low levels of cases of incest reported to the police or processed by magistrate and higher courts. Between the period 1995 to 1999 inclusively, the researchers identified a total of 13 cases of incest from police records in all areas studied. Out of this number, ten cases were from police records in greater Gaborone and three from greater Francistown. Table 1 summarises the cases reported to the police by year and area of study. The low levels in reported cases realised by this study are consistent with those documented by a study focusing on rape commissioned by the Department of Police in the Office of the State President. The study by the police examined dockets of various forms of crimes against morality, including those of incest and defilement, in 25 police stations located in rural and urban areas in the south, south-central and northern parts of the country over a period of three years, from 1996 to 1998. But only two cases of incest reported to the police were identified (Botswana Police, 1999).

The dismally low number of cases that find their way to the courts compounds the problem of under-reporting of cases of incest further. For the five-year period covered by this study, the researchers only identified one case of incest that had been lodged with the magistrate court in Francistown. This left the research team wondering what could have happened to the other 12 cases reported to the police during the same period. Discussions with the police revealed that after investigating incest cases they referred them to the Attorney General's Chambers for approval to prosecute. According to them they referred most of the reported cases to the Attorney General's Chambers but they had no idea what happened to them once they reached there.

Section 171 of the Penal Code provides that no cases of incest are prosecuted without written consent from the Attorney General's Chambers. According to the office of the Attorney General, the rationale for this provision is informed by the fact that the offence of incest is controversial and brings conflict between members of a family. It is therefore pertinent to assess the strengths of the case and establish if there is enough proof or evidence to prosecute. The

TABLE 1: CASES OF INCEST REPORTED TO THE POLICE BY AREA OF STUDY, 1995–1999

Year	Greater Gaborone	Greater Francistown	Total
1995	2	0	2
1996	0	1	1
1997	0	0	0
1998	7	2	9
1999	1	0	1
Total	10	3	13

office further indicated that they were faced with the following problems in prosecuting cases of incest:

- ☞ Often the cases of incest are reported long after the incidents happened, and when most of the physical evidence has been destroyed.
- ☞ The legal system also takes time in prosecuting the cases and so there is a backlog of cases. This results in some victims and their parents changing their minds about prosecuting as the anger subsides over time. They usually come up with excuses such as *'ngwana o ne a lora'*, meaning that the child was only dreaming, that nothing of the sort actually happened. Even where the medical report provides evidence, parents usually claim that *'ke balekane ba gagwe'*, meaning that the child had been having sexual intercourse with her age mates.
- ☞ Most of the time, mothers of victims do not want to continue with the cases of incest to preserve their marriages, for opportunistic and materialistic reasons. The respondent at the Attorney General's Chambers stated that 'This Setswana saying that *mmangwana o tshwara thipa ka fa bogaleng* (a mother would protect her child with her own life), is a fallacy'.

In the light of the above problems, most of the incest cases referred to the Attorney General's Chambers by police for consent to prosecute fizzled out before they reached the trial stage.

5.1 Possible Explanations of Under-reporting

Incest is far more common than anyone has been able to document (Cleveland, 1986) mainly due to the under-reporting of the offence. Accurate statistics are impossible to attain and its true extent remains unknown. There are several possible explanations for the under-reporting on incest. One such explanation would be the secrecy surrounding the problem. Incestuous relationships are viewed as controversial and sensitive. The perpetrators are often close relatives of the victim and consequently there is a stigma associated with the commission of the offence. It is precisely because of this stigma that victims prefer to remain silent about it. This view is shared by Hunt and Kitzinger (1996) who point out that cases of incest are often under-reported because, in addition to the stigma, reporting them may bring tension and misunderstanding among relatives or members of the same family.

The situation in Botswana is not much different. The extent of abuse of women and girl-children by men is not adequately documented. This is the case because, generally speaking, domestic violence is rarely reported to law enforcement authorities. Where reporting occurs, the police tend to treat it as a private matter and not as a criminal offence like other forms of violence. Speaking with reference to incest, the tribal leaders interviewed for this, for example, indicated that they sometimes know of incest offences occurring in their villages but which are not reported to them or anywhere else. This, they explained, was done to avoid the stigma that is attached to such offences once they come into the public eye. In doing so, the involved parties also sought to protect their 'pride and dignity' and avoid any embarrassment to the family. They asserted that most of these cases are 'solved at the family level'.

Other key informants of the study expressed similar views. According to them, incest is widely committed, but because of the shame and social stigma associated with it, such cases often remained within the family. Consistent with the tribal leaders, they argued that the inclination to protect the integrity and reputation of the family inevitably resulted in family members deciding to keep quiet. However, it should be noted that, as Cleveland (1986) pointed out, elevating incest to the status of a forbidden subject does not prevent it from happening. Rather, it simply prevents it from being recognised as a problem. The wall of silence surrounding the offence of incest has tended to downplay the magnitude of the problem and to undermine the seriousness with which society ought to treat it.

A second explanation of the under-reporting of incest offences is the refusal by societal members to believe that it is happening. The abused child often becomes 'the victim nobody believes' because no one wants to believe that incest can occur (Justice and Justice, 1979). Victims thus experience a fear of not being believed by family members, and that prevents them from reporting the offence. The tendency for family member is, not to believe an incest victim, particularly in those cases where the offender is also the breadwinner for the victim's family. In many such cases the dependency of the family on an income earner outweighs the interests of the child to be protected from sexual abuse.

The failure to report some incidences of incest may be explained in terms of the inferior economic, legal and social status of women in their families and communities. This renders them incapable of protecting their daughters from abuse, and increases the daughters' vulnerability to abuse including (incestuous) sexual exploitation. Where such abuse actually occurs, mothers are, more often than not, unwilling to report it or even talk about it. The interests of the family override the interests of the victim and the protection of her/his rights. The burden of reporting the abuse to the authorities is left to the victim who already suffers feelings of shame, guilt and low self-esteem and is thus unlikely to do so. This may be encouraging to the offenders who continue their abusive acts and scar more innocent lives.

Incest, like most other forms of family violence, also reflects power relations that favour males. It is a form of domination of the perpetrator over the victim. According to feminists, in patriarchal societies women are considered to be men's property and children 'wholly owned subsidiaries' (Van der Mey and Neff, 1986:38). Those who support this view argue that abusers continue the incest pattern because they want to feel power over the victims; they feel strong and in control. Victims, on the other hand, submit to the power of the perpetrator and consequently fail to report the offence to law enforcement authorities. In some cases the perpetrator may even threaten to harm the victim if he or she reports the incident. This creates a fear of reprisal which causes many victims to be reluctant to report incidents of incest.

The incidence of incest and, one may conclude, the failure to report it, is also linked to the way children are socialised. The findings of this study, for instance, revealed a disturbing submissiveness of girl-children to male sexual advances. The responses of the girl-children to such sexual advances by adult males who are blood relatives, and to whom they are supposed to look up to for protection, can be confusing, baffling. This is likely to be the case where one is not familiar with the Setswana socialization of children, particularly as pertains to their relationships with adults. Setswana traditional culture, which is still very much alive for the majority of Batswana, teaches children to obey adults whether they are relatives or not. They are supposed to 'respect' and not to question them. The girl-child is brought up to view assertiveness as a sign of disrespect towards her elders, and consequently she is not equipped with the proper skills to assert and protect herself. In addition, children have an innocent unwavering trust, especially in male adults. Some men take advantage of this situation to perpetrate abuse, knowing that, due to their age, their young victims will most likely trust them and hence go along with anything they suggest.

That socialization can contribute to the prevalence of incest was illustrated by some of the victims' statements to the police which were examined by this study. Few as these might have been, they revealed the form of submissiveness of girls to male sexual advances associated with the above socialization. According to the statements, offenders simply held their victims by the wrists, pulled them into a hut/house or towards a bed, and then asked them to undress, which they did. Many of the statements by the victims read thus: 'He then asked me to lie down and he inserted his penis inside my vagina'. It is disheartening to note that none of the statements indicated any attempt by the victims to fight off the offenders or to scream or to ask what they intended to do with them. The statements give the impression that the victims simply complied with what they were told to do without any fuss.

5.2 Knowledge and Views about Incest

Knowledge about the legal definition of incest, procedures for seeking legal remedies, and penalties varied depending on the informants. Data was collected from students, doctors, traditional leaders and magistrates through group discussions and workshops.

5.2.1 Secondary School Students

As discussed in the methodology chapter, a brainstorming technique was employed as a strategy to find out the understanding by secondary school students of the concept of incest, without interrupting their thought processes or influencing their responses. Asked to brainstorm on the definition of incest the students gave the following responses:

- ☞ sexual intercourse;
- ☞ abuse;
- ☞ ancestors;
- ☞ tradition;
- ☞ parents;

- child abuse;
- children;
- secret;
- religion; and
- Christianity.

Asked to define the concept of incest in view of their responses during the brainstorming session the students gave the following responses:

- two members of the same family having a sexual relationship;
- any two members of the same family related by blood (such as a mother and her son) having a sexual relationship;
- people related having an intimate relationship;
- sexual relationship between blood relations;
- intimate relationship between two people who are related;
- when a child is raped by his/her parent in a cunning manner; and
- siblings playing *mantlwane*[5], playing the role of parents leads to incest; that is, siblings acting like parents which can lead to incest.

Following the brainstorming session, the researchers gave the students the Penal Code definition of incest, and participants compared and contrasted the legal definition with their own. Some students expressed dissatisfaction with, and others horror at, the Penal Code definition of incest. They considered the legal definition to be inadequate in that it left out some people whom students felt should be included within the purview of the definition of the offence. According to the students, it is 'mostly step-fathers, maternal uncles, cousins and fathers' who are guilty of incestuous relationships. In particular they singled out maternal uncles as the worst perpetrators of incest because *'ba batla ditlhogo'*, they want gifts which, according to some Setswana customary practices, maternal uncles are entitled to from their nephews and nieces.

In some Setswana tribal groups, a maternal uncle plays a very important role in the lives of his nieces and nephews. Whereas Setswana custom prescribes that the father is the ultimate decision-maker and guardian of the children, in some groups and for certain purposes, fathers cannot finalise certain decisions without the participation of maternal uncles, particularly the eldest uncle (WLSA, 1992). This was and is so because customarily a woman does

---

[5] *'Mantlwane'* is the same as playing house.

not actively participate in the 'public sphere', nor is she to be seen to be having any decision-making powers even in matters concerning her own children. Where her point of view regarding her children is required, particularly during rites of passage such as births, weddings and death, she is heard through her brothers, the *bomalome* – maternal uncles to her children.

The woman's brothers are her spokespersons and they negotiate and bargain on her behalf. *Bomalome* are said to be *ditlhogo*, literally meaning 'heads'. They are heads with eyes to see, ears to hear and mouths to speak on behalf of their sisters. Custom prescribes that, from time to time, the maternal uncle be rewarded for the important role he plays in the lives of his nephews and nieces. The reward comes in the form of material presents such as a cow or goat. Such reward bears the same name as the uncles, *ditlhogo*. It is here submitted that where the uncle negotiates sex with his niece in place of *ditlhogo* it is corruption of Setswana customary practices. This corruption has, over the years, been reinforced by one of the most popular Setswana songs entitled 'Malala Swii'. Part of the song goes as follows:

Setlogolo ntsha ditlhogo	Niece/nephew present me with a gift
Ditlhogo tsa eng malome?	What kind of gift, uncle?
Sengwe le sengwe ke ditlhogo	Any form of gift is acceptable
Serope le sone ditlhogo.	Even the thigh can be a gift.

There are clearly sexual connotations in the song that every Motswana understands. S*erope* is a thigh and here it implies sexual intercourse.

According to the students, fathers and uncles make certain excuses to justify why they have sexual intercourse with their daughters and nieces. One of the reasons they gave was that the offenders claimed that *'ba tiisa mokwatla'*, literally meaning that they are strengthening the child's (victim's) back, implying that they are physically training and preparing the child for her role as a sexual partner to her future husband. This justification reinforces the patriarchy and power theory that women and girl-children exist with and for men; that they are perceived first and foremost as sexual objects.

Another most commonly used excuse is embodied in the statement *'ba roba se ba se jwadileng'*, literally meaning that they reap what they sow. The implication here is that the adult offenders have invested in the upbringing of the victim and hence feel they have to benefit from their contribution. Again, this perception further reinforces the patriarchy and power theory that girl-children and women are perceived as property from which to gain and not as human beings with independent existence. The students also gave cases in which fathers impregnate their daughters, where the father would say *'ke go direla phoso ngwanaka, mmago ga ayo'*, literally meaning that, although what I'm doing is wrong, my daughter, your mother is not around, to justify sleeping with the daughter. Students explained that this was common when the mother was at *masimo* (the farm area) for some time or at a funeral. It is on the basis of these justifications that the students felt very strongly that the definition of incest should be expanded to incorporate other extended family members who have not been included in the Penal Code definition such as maternal and paternal aunts, uncles, cousins, ste-parents, ste-brothers and step-sisters.

Much as the students interviewed understood the concept of incest, they would not necessarily report it when it took place. Some students indicated that sometimes their mothers did not believe them when they informed them that their fathers or uncles abused them sexually. Data has revealed that the mother often accuses the girl of lying about the allegations of incest. And where the matter is reported to the police, the parent, particularly the mother, withdraws the case to settle the matter at family level. This conduct is sometimes explained by the fact that the father is the breadwinner and taking him to task for his conduct may have serious economic consequences for the family. This therefore leaves women, especially those who are dependent on their husbands, with no choice but to adopt a withdrawal strategy for survival purposes.

Some students from Tutume and Gaborone were strongly opposed to the five-year penalty for incest saying it is too long and severe. Their explanation was that the penalty should only apply if there was no agreement between the father/uncle and the girl. Tutume students explained that *'O kgona go dumela malomaago kana rrago'*, meaning, 'you are able to agree to sleep with your uncle or your father'. They explained the following scenario:

> **Uncle:** *Setlogolo kana ke a diila,* meaning, "niece I am suffering' [because I have no woman].
> **Niece:** '*Malome, le nna ke a diila. Re tlaa thusanya ka gore ga ke na mosimane yoo nkgatlhegelang,* meaning, 'Uncle I'm also suffering. Let us help each other because I cannot find a male who wants me'.

Some of the students explained that, *'Gape fa o itse gore rrago o go tshodisitse ngwana o tlhokomelela ngwana wa gago mo lapeng'*, that is, it is better if it's your father who has made you pregnant, because he will support and look after your child.

5.2.2 Tribal Leaders and Administrators

According to the Penal Code, cases of incest do not fall within the jurisdiction of tribal leaders and administrators. Such types of cases are prosecuted at the magistrate courts. Nevertheless, the study sought the opinions of tribal leaders and administrators concerning incest, as well as examining cases of *tshenyo* (seduction) to find out if any such cases involved girls who had been impregnated by their blood relatives. The discussion held with this cadre of leaders and administrators focused on the existing laws dealing with incest, the handling of such offences through traditional customs, and the procedures and punitive measures available at the *kgotla*, the customary courts.

The traditional leaders admitted that incest did indeed occur and that women who had found their husbands (fathers or stepfathers of the children), uncles and cousins (of the children) sexually violating these children would 'secretly' report the matter to the tribal authorities – if they reported at all. According to them, women are the ones who are most likely to notice any peculiar incidences that would suggest the existence of incestuous relationships in the family. However, the particulars of such relationships are likely to remain hidden and to be dealt with discreetly because the women who report them to the tribal authorities only request the authorities to intervene by 'talking to the perpetrator' with a view to forcing him to stop abusing the children. They are not interested in getting the perpetrator punished. The reason as to why the women, particularly those who are married, are only interested in the perpetrator being forced to stop the abuse and not in any punitive measures is because they fear *'go ithubela malapa'*, breaking their marriages. These women want the incestuous relationship to come to an end, but they are not willing to leave the husband and take the children away from him. The tribal authorities emphasised that the women's unwillingness to leave the husband comes about as a result of the state of financial dependence that the women and their children have on the man.

In addition, data showed that sometimes the police referred cases of incest to tribal leaders at the *kgotla* for arbitration even though they knew that customary courts had no jurisdiction to hear cases of incest. This occurred because police officers are socially involved with the community they police. They tend to understand and promote negotiations and reconciliation as opposed to prosecution and, as a result, perpetuate male domination. However, the tribal leaders did not disclose how they resolved such cases. Their reluctance may have been influenced by the fact that they were aware that they had no jurisdiction over such offences.

The tribal leaders, and especially chiefs, strongly felt that cases of incest should be under their jurisdiction. They also expressed displeasure with the dual system of justice administration, arguing that customary courts in some instances have adopted western culture and this makes it difficult and confusing in the application of the law. It was evident that most chiefs and headmen had little understanding of the general law and the concepts associated with it. The discussions, however, provided some useful insights into the issue of incest by revealing that traditional leaders viewed incest in terms of the customary values and beliefs of their tribal group.

Asked to provide a Setswana term for incest, the tribal leaders in all research areas failed to produce any and asserted that such a word did not exist in the Setswana vocabulary. According to them, one could only describe the act. Invariably, they referred to incest as *botlhodi*, evil. Some explained that having sexual intercourse with one's child was *boloi*, witchcraft. The disgust with which some of the traditional leaders regarded the act of incest was captured in the metaphors they used such as '*go ija motlhana*', which literally translated means to eat one's placenta.

The tribal leaders explained that 'in the old days' punishment for incest was '*go mo lobela dintshi*', meaning punishment by death. Often the village chief would commission the regiment of the man who had committed such an offence to go for a hunting expedition and on the return of the regiment the man would be said to have been eaten by lions. They expressed regret that unfortunately these days the issue of *ditshwanelo*, human rights, prevents leaders from taking such action. However, they suggested that such an offender should be publicly humiliated by holding his trial and administering corporal punishment at the *kgotla* where every member of the village could attend.

On the issue of the Penal Code definition of incest, the tribal leaders and administrators felt that, as it stood, it was too exclusionist. They expressed the concern that it was based on the Western concept of the nuclear family. Thus, it should be expanded to include other family members like maternal uncles and aunts, stepparents and other blood relatives. Some of the participants, however, strongly felt that cousins should not be included because there are certain tribes where it is permissible to marry one's cousin. To rationalise the inclusion of stepfathers among those relations listed in the Penal Code, the tribal leaders and administrators argued that in 'Setswana culture' when a man marries a woman who already has a child then that child becomes his as well. They asserted that excluding such a man from the definition of incest thus encourages it.

It is important to contextualise the position adopted by some of the tribal leaders that the definition of incest should not include cousins. In Setswana, the brother of one's father is referred to as either younger father or older father, and not uncle. Similarly, one's mother's sister is referred to as younger mother or older mother, and not aunt. Children of brothers, like those of sisters, are considered siblings and not cousins. Hence sexual relations between them is prohibited. On the other hand, the brother of one's mother is referred to as *malome* (meaning maternal uncle), regardless of whether he is younger or older than one's mother. The sister of one's father is referred to as *rakgadi*, (meaning aunt) regardless of whether she is younger or older than one's father. Children of a brother and sister are *bontsala* (cousins). Hence in some tribes, cousins can marry.

Within the context described above, cousins, referring to children of a brother and a sister, have a special relationship. They are expected to look out for each other's interests, to protect and defend one another. They also have a teasing relationship, *baa tlhagana*. The teasing comes in many forms including joking, making fun of one another, flirting and touching. Even as minors, when one cousin complains to a parent that they don't like the way the other is making fun of them they are told, *'Ke ntsalao, otlaa seka kae?'* meaning that s/he is your cousin, you cannot take him/her to court. In line with customary socialization, the flirting is, for the most part, initiated by males towards their female cousins and is a lifelong form of interaction. It is not unusual for a male to negotiate sex with his female cousin but she is at liberty to reject or accept such advances. Some of the tribal leaders, however, did not condone sexual relationships between such cousins. Their grounds were that the progeny of such a union would have genetic aberrations – a fact, which has been scientifically proven. It is suggested here that, even though customary socialization allows one the choice to accept or turn down sexual advances by another, such customary practices encourage sexual harassment which in turn promote incestuous relationships.

In the kind of relationship described above, male and female cousins are referred to as *'monna le mosadi'* meaning husband and wife. They may actually marry, as captured by the Setswana saying which goes, *'Ngwana wa ga malome nnyala 'kgomo di boele sakeng'*, that is, 'my uncle's [maternal] child, marry me, so that the cattle [for *lobola*] remain within the family'. But in Masunga and Tutume chiefs and headmen frowned upon this practice. They exclaimed with shock, *'Ini,? Mwana wa basekulu bangu?!'*, that is, 'What? My uncle's child?' They emphasised that such behaviour was taboo among the Bakalanga. However, other informants in Tutume, especially school students, expressed a divergent view, claiming that such sexual relationships did actually happen. This shows that what was expressed by the tribal authorities may well have been eroded with time and no longer obtains in the present era.

5.3 The Perpetrators and Victims of Incest

According to the data realised by this study, in all cases of incest males are the perpetrators while young females are the victims. The study revealed that some biological fathers sexually abuse their daughters. Stepfathers also abuse their stepdaughters, as do paternal and maternal uncles, cousins and other relatives. These findings are consistent with those of the 1999 police study on rape which found that 13% of the perpetrators of the sexual abuse cases reported to the police included stepfathers, cousins, uncles, and nephews (Botswana Police, 1999:33-34). They also support the revelation by Spies (1992) that, more often than not, incest happens to young girls who are abused by their fathers, stepfathers, grandfathers or uncles. According to Spies, incest between brothers and sisters, fathers and sons, or mothers and sons was less common. However, based on existing evidence, boys do not report incest as much as girls (Spies, 1992; Renvoize, 1982).

5.3.1 Biological Fathers and Step-fathers

Both police and some NGO records examined for this study revealed that biological fathers do sexually abuse their daughters. The case studies which follow are illustrative.

Case study 1: Mma Gaone
A divorced mother of five visited WLSA offices seeking help for her children whom, she alleged, were being sexually abused by their biological father. At the time of divorce the husband was granted custody of the younger children. The elderly children moved in with their mother. Her husband continued sharing his bed with the children and molesting them for some time after the divorce. A doctor later diagnosed the youngest daughter, aged eight years, as having a sexually transmitted disease. The girl was also said to have a history of sexual relations. This was discovered when the children were visiting their mother during school holidays. The father disowned one of the daughters, aged thirteen years because, the mother claimed, she asserted herself and refused to continue sleeping with him. The girl went to live with her mother.

The mother also alleged that her ex-husband had also molested the other daughter, aged seventeen. Later, in an attempt to put an end to the abuse, the 17-year-old arranged for the domestic helper to sleep in her father's bed instead of her. That same day she sneaked her boyfriend into the house. When her father discovered this he beat her and the boyfriend. After the beatings the girl attempted to end her life but was rescued by the domestic helper. The son in the family has been affected by this so much that he wants nothing to do with the family. All the time the mother was relating the story, she was crying.

Case study 2: Dawn
Dawn is 19 years old. Her father had sexually abused her and her sisters over a period of several years. The father did not allow them to have any friends and ensured that they spend all their free time with him. When she was posted to a village in the north for her Tirelo Sechaba (National Service), she thought that she had escaped. Unfortunately the father insisted that she should visit him every weekend in a town where he worked. If she did not join him, he took the trip to the village to pick her up. Dawn eventually consulted some peer educators and social workers who referred her to one NGO which assisted her in finding a place to stay during police investigations. Her father was eventually arrested but not before her mother requested that she be returned home. He eventually committed suicide.

Stepfathers have also been identified as sexual abusers of their stepdaughters. In some instances the abuse may be condoned by the mothers of the abused children as evident from the case study presented below.

Case study 3: Naledi
Naledi, a 17-year-old girl, was doing her National Service at a junior secondary school in one of the villages. She had decided to spend her holidays at her maternal grandmother's home in the same district where she did her National Service instead of going home to her parents. When her stepfather realised that she was not coming home, he threatened to go and get her. She went to the social workers in the area and explained her predicament to them; that earlier her stepfather had sexually abused her and as a result she did not want to go home.

The social workers informed the researchers that there was no policy protecting them in the course of their work if they took such matters further for legal action. Eventually they sought the opinion of Naledi's mother who insisted that her daughter should come home as summoned by her stepfather. She insisted that 'I am an adult woman. I've been with many men in my life and this is the only one who wanted to marry me. So, I want the girl back home.'

All three case studies presented above demonstrate the manifestations of patriarchy in our society with the result that some men believe that they have the right to dominate and control the lives of women and girls, particularly those within their families. Such men perceive women as objects for satisfying their sexual desires. Some women, as illustrated by Case study 3, reinforce this patriarchal control. In this case Naledi's mother was aware of the sexual relationship between her husband and her daughter but chose to support her husband to save her marriage.

5.3.2 Brothers

The findings of the study also revealed that some brothers abuse their sisters. This was evident from a case examined from one of the NGOs studied. According to this case, a 14-year-old girl had been abused sexually by her 21-year-old brother. He had sneaked upon her at night while she was sleeping. The girl fell pregnant and had a baby boy. She is currently back at school. The brother was still awaiting trial at the time of data collection.

5.3.3 Maternal Uncles

Discussions with tribal leaders and school children revealed that maternal uncles sexually abuse their nieces. The case study presented below testifies to this fact.

Case study 4: Malome
A 17-year-old male had sex with his three-year-old niece while the mother was away from home. She had left her brother baby sitting for her. The 14-year-old brother of the perpetrator found him sexually abusing the child in the bathroom. The perpetrator's statement to the police reads thus:

> She [the victim] told me she was sweating and she wanted me to bathe her. After bathing her, I picked her from the bath and put her on the floor. I pulled down my trousers to my thighs. I put her on the floor on her back. I had closed the bathroom door. My intention was to have sex with her. I took my penis out and tried to insert it into her vagina, but I could not. I was supporting my penis with my left hand so that it could not miss her private parts. I ejaculated. After having sex with her, I opened the bathroom door and went out.

Part of the statement to the police by the younger brother to the offender reads thus:

> I was at home with Modiri and Lorato. Lorato is my niece and is three and half years old. Modiri and Lorato were in the bathroom. After a while I went outside to wash my blankets. As I was washing, I decided to take a piece of wood near the

bathroom window. I saw Modiri (17 years), my elder brother and Lorato, my niece, lying on the floor inside the bathroom. Modiri was lying on top of Lorato. I saw Modiri moving his buttocks up and down many times. I did not say anything, as I was surprised. Modiri did not see me. I went back to washing my blankets. After a while I went back to the window. I saw Modiri and Lorato bathing together.

The medical doctor's remarks following examination of the child revealed that her vaginal opening was 'easy'. The case was reported in March 1998 and was withdrawn in January 2000. The child's mother withdrew the case because, as she informed the police: 'Since then he [the perpetrator] has shown signs of responsibility and co-operation. He is helping my mother in taking care of the family. My parents also talked to him and he has reformed'.

There are other examples that are consistent with Case study 4 above. One such case involved a young girl aged 14 years. She reported that her uncle had asked her to go and help clean his house and do his laundry. When she was bending over the bathtub washing the clothes the uncle came up from behind *'a bo a e latlhela mo teng'*, that is, shoved his penis into her vagina. Another case involved a 16-year-old girl who was sexually abused by her 53-year-old uncle. The girl reported that her uncle had sexual intercourse with her on four occasions without using a condom. She fell pregnant and when the case came before the police he subsequently committed suicide.

It should be noted that, as alluded to earlier in previous sections, offences involving uncles are not legally recognised as incestuous relationships but rather defilement as in any sexual encounter with an underage person, even though there is a close proximity along bloodlines.

5.4 Factors Promoting Incest

Three factors were identified by some of the respondents of our study to be the major promoters of incest in society. These are poverty, the existence of blended families (see below, 5.4.2) and the desire by women to maintain a male-centred status quo.

5.4.1 Poverty

Both the police and the students identified poverty as one of the factors contributing to incest. They indicated that often the offending adult is also the breadwinner. If he is reported to law enforcement authorities he may go to prison and the family would be left with no one to support them. In some cases, the offender acts as a guardian of the victim, living with her in his home. This usually occurs where the parents are too poor to educate or maintain their child. Therefore, to enable her to attend school, they entrust her to a blood relative who is financially better off. In situations of single mothers, such guardians are often maternal uncles who, according to Setswana traditional culture, are obliged to take care of their unmarried sisters' children. In some situations such arrangements have been found to be dangerous because the victim may opt not to report the abuse for fear of losing financial support or of seeming ungrateful. This may result in repeated abuse. A case depicting such a scenario appeared on page seven of the *Midweek Sun* newspaper, 8 April 1998 edition. The article reported on a case where the parents of a sexually abused girl lived from hand to mouth through subsistence agriculture and selling *phane* worms. For her to go to school, the parents entrusted her to her more financially advantaged maternal uncle and continued to stay with him, despite his known sexual abuse against her.

5.4.2 Blended Families

Blended families, also referred to as compounded or melded families, are mainly the result of remarriage after divorce/separation. They represent families in which at least one parent has been previously married. A blended family includes children from one or both of those marriages (Johnson, 1995). As such, it is characterised by a complicated system of blood relations between parents and children; sometimes one family may be characterised by two sets of step-relationships simultaneously. Blended families, for example, may include stepfathers/mothers, stepchildren, stepsisters/brothers and cohabiting boyfriends–girlfriends. Because of the high rates of divorce and subsequent remarriage blended families are on the rise in most societies (Newman, 1995). In Botswana the factor of divorce/separation is currently compounded further by the high percentage of children born to single women. When these women eventually get married or enter into a cohabitation relationship, the man, in most cases, takes on the care of the children. In some cases the man sexually molests his partner's children. Furthermore, he may justify his behaviour by stating that they are not his biological children.

The tendency for blended families to promote incest is evident in a newspaper article which profiled an incident whereby a stepfather defiled his 15-year-old stepdaughter, then murdered her: Part of the article read thus *(Botswana Guardian*, 24 January 1997:1):

> Police have launched a hunt for a man, Andy Koitsiwe, 40 years, who allegedly

raped his 15-year-old stepdaughter and strangled her to death in Tlokweng. The girl, who completed her Junior Certificate last year, was found murdered in the family's rented house, lying on a blood-stained mattress. She had been sexually assaulted then strangled, judging from the bruises found around her neck. Koitsiwe had also opened a domestic gas cylinder to allow gas to fill the room. Police suspect that he wanted to make it look like the victim had committed suicide. The aggrieved mother of the victim, Seanokeng Moilwe, 31 years, said there had been a strange incident at home recently in which Koitsiwe had attempted to stab the children with a kitchen knife while they were sleeping. 'He had never done that kind of thing to them before', she said. 'He later apologised'.

5.4.3 Desire to Maintain the Status Quo

According to the tribal leaders interviewed for this study, many women prefer to remain silent or keep the crime of incest a family secret. The majority of the cases remained within the family in an attempt by family members to avoid stigmatization of that family by the rest of the community members. In effect what happens is the protection of the family's good name at the expense of the rights, happiness and health of the abused. Our research revealed a strong desire by the women to keep the matter secret, claiming that it had been amicably solved at family level.

The findings of this study are consistent with Cleveland's (1986) argument that, although incest has existed throughout the ages and is found in all known cultures, it is an emotionally charged subject carrying strong cultural taboos. It is forbidden and prohibited by every culture and is treated as so abominable that it must not be thought about or discussed. Incest thus tends to remain a family secret. The only time it comes out is when the victim self-reports, the perpetrator is in jail usually for other offences, the victim develops behavioural problems and professional help is sought, or when the victim becomes pregnant as a result of the incestuous relationship.

THE INCIDENCE OF DEFILEMENT

Previous studies show that in Botswana there is a high rate of teenage pregnancies of girl-children aged between 15 and 18 years (WLSA, 1992; Central Statistics Office, 1999). Based on the Ministry of Education statistics (Central Statistics Office, 1997: xiii), of the 3287 secondary school dropouts[6] 1259 were as a result of pregnancy. The majority of the girls drop out during the first three years of their secondary school education. This points to the high rate of defilement in Botswana.

6.1 The Extent of Defilement

To assess the prevalence of defilement in Botswana, the study examined records from police stations for the period 1994 to 1999. In greater Gaborone records from Central, Old Naledi, Broadhurst, Mogoditshane and Mochudi police stations were analysed, while in greater Francistown, records from Tatitown, Kutlwano, Masunga, Tutume and Tonota police stations were examined. The results for the six-year period covered by the study are summarised under Table 2 overleaf. As is evident from the table, there are relatively low levels of cases of persons charged with the offence of defilement at police stations. These figures, however, are rather misleading because they represent only those cases that the police categorised as defilement. Through careful examination of all cases classified as 'offences against morality' the researchers identified an additional 160 cases of defilement whereby the accused were charged with the offence of rape. Of this number, 72 were in the greater Gaborone area while 88 were in the greater Francistown area. This brought the total number of defilement cases identified for the period 1995 to 1999 to 254.

The seemingly low cases of defilement can be attributed to the problem of classification of such sexual offences by the police. The police often classified a significant number of defilement cases as rape. In practice they often treated

---

6   Secondary school in Botswana covers a period of five years. On the average the entry age is 13 years.

TABLE 2: CASES OF DEFILEMENT REPORTED TO THE POLICE BY YEAR AND RESEARCH AREA

Year	Greater Gaborone	Greater Francistown	Total
1994	5	0	5
1995	3	0	3
1996	9	3	12
1997	16	10	26
1998	22	18	40
1999	5	3	8
Total	**60**	**34**	**94**

some cases of defilement as rape if they concluded that the victim had not 'consented' to sexual intercourse. Case study 5 below is illustrative.

Case study 5: Neo and Peo
Two girls, both aged six years, were playing in a yard at a cattle post. An adult male was drinking *chibuku* in the same yard. As he was leaving at around eight p.m., he dragged the two girls to a nearby bush and sexually abused them. The parents later reported the case to the police and the man was arrested and charged with two counts of rape. The medical report indicated that the victims' private parts were bruised. The accused was convicted and sentenced to eight years imprisonment for count one and to six years imprisonment for count two. The sentences were to run concurrently.

Legally, the case presented above is a clear one of defilement. Yet the justice system treated it as rape and the accused was convicted of the same. On the other hand, where there was 'consent', the police classified the charge as defilement, such as when the victim and the perpetrator were said to be or had been lovers as indicated in the case study below.

Case study 6: Mmatiro
Mmatiro, the complainant, found her daughter aged 12 years old, at around

three a.m. in the toilet within the yard with a male aged 21 years old, a regular customer at her shebeen. She suspected them of having had sex and reported the matter to the police. The accused admitted that they have been sleeping together for the past 5 months. The medical records indicated that the complainant's daughter was sexually active. The accused was charged with defilement of girls under the age of 16 years. The case was however withdrawn three days later, after being reported to the police by the complainant, giving the following reason:'I know the accused's mother very well. The matter will be discussed at home'.

The research team faced the difficulty of sifting rape from cases of defilement as the police tended to prosecute cases of defilement as if they were rape. The tendency by the police to classify defilement as rape can be confusing to a researcher, but the researchers were informed that it is done for strategic reasons. Technically, where a charge of defilement may not succeed, a rape charge is preferred instead of the offender going unpunished. This is so because technically the elements that ought to be proved in a defilement case are not the same as rape. For instance, where the police prosecute for defilement, it is absolutely imperative to prove the age of the victim. If such is not proven the charge collapses in its entirety. Tactically, it may then be proper to prosecute for rape where age is not necessarily an essential ingredient of the offence.

Of the cases that are reported to the police, few are successfully prosecuted. This was due to the high frequency of case withdrawals, police mistakes and absconding.

6.1.1 Withdrawal of Cases

Some complainants withdrew cases at the police stations and claimed to have settled the matter at family level. For instance, a mother lodged a complaint with the police that her 15 years old daughter was sexually involved with a man aged 30 years. The accused was actually caught defiling the victim. On arrival at the police station, the victim made a written statement requesting for the case to be withdrawn. The reasons for withdrawal were cited as her 'unwillingness to take the accused to court [as] the accused had proposed love to me and I accepted'. What was fascinating in this particular case was that the victim's parents supported her request for withdrawal arguing that 'a trial would psychologically affect their child who was still young and in school'. To this statement they added, 'the matter has been resolved between the two families at home'. The police consequently withdrew the case.

Under criminal law, cases of defilement are an offence against the state and as such cannot be withdrawn by the complainants. However, the police officers, like the complainants, have been socialised according to Setswana customs and values to recognise and encourage negotiation and reconciliation of disputes especially at family level. The police therefore, at times, find themselves in a dilemma where complainants seek to withdraw such cases which otherwise are considered crimes against the state and not the individual. The dilemma they find themselves in is a reflection of legal pluralism in operation whereby both general law, rules and regulations are in competition with customary laws and practices. It must also be mentioned that much as permitting cases to be withdrawn may be a feature of socialization, in some cases it is a reflection of inadequate training. It is worth noting that at the time of data collection, however, the Commissioner of the Botswana Police service had issued a directive to the effect that no such cases be withdrawn at the police level at the request of the complainants.

Another basis for withdrawal or closure of cases is insufficient evidence. The data showed that decisions based on insufficient evidence raised a lot of questions that border on the miscarriage of justice. For instance, most cases were closed due to 'insufficient evidence' against the accused. More often than not, it was unclear on what basis the evidence was judged to be too insignificant to implicate the accused. This is illustrated by the case study below.

Case study 7: Bosupi
At three p.m. an 11-year-old girl was coming from her teacher's house where she had been sent to take exercise books. A 35-year-old man who was known to her raped her. He was a person she knew in the neighbourhood. He called out to her and she ignored him. After that he pulled her to the bushes and flashed a knife, strangled her and raped her.

The complainant was taken to hospital and to forensic laboratory for analysis. The results of the medical report were as follows:

Sex life:	Not active
Menstruation:	Nil
Assault:	Bruised left eye
Hymen:	Ruptured
Pereneum:	Small tear
Discharge:	Around labia majora
Haemorrhage:	Around vaginal orifice
Examination:	Painful
Verdict by doctor:	Fresh rape

Although the perpetrator was a well-known criminal who had a previous conviction of attempted rape where he was given six years in prison and six strokes, the police records showed the following:

(a) The investigating officer suggested that the case be closed because of insufficient evidence because the affidavit from the forensic analyst revealed that there was no spermatozoa identified from the vaginal swabs.
(b) The suspect was apprehended and brought in from Lobatse and detained in police custody.
(c) The accused was arrested, warned, cautioned and charged. Accused detained in police custody. Forensic lab affidavit attached to docket.
(d) Accused did not appear (he was given bail by the magistrate court). Applied for warrant of arrest, because the accused never turned up.
(e) Station commander suggests that when an accused disappears a case is withdrawn under Section 150(4) of Criminal Procedure and Evidence (CP&E) Act.

Consequently the case was withdrawn by the public prosecutor under section 150 of CP&E for insufficient evidence.

What the above case clearly shows is that there is the need to improve the capacity of the police to gather evidence. Gathering evidence is a skill that has to be acquired. If this capacity is not improved, substantial miscarriage of justice will inevitably result.

6.1.2 Police Mistakes
Though very hard working, police sometimes make mistakes, and at other times can be careless. One case, for instance, was closed because an officer had been negligent and extremely indolent. He found used condoms at the scene of the crime where the victim had directed him. He only took this piece of evidence to the forensic lab 'after some days' only to be told that not only had the sperm dried, but that it was also rotten. The case was closed on the basis of 'insufficient evidence' and the accused got away.

6.1.3 Absconding
Some cases are closed because either the accused or the key witness, the victim herself, absconds. The following case illustrates this tendency.

Case study 8: Jackie
A 16-year-old girl was asleep at midnight in a yard where her girlfriend stayed.

A man came into the room that did not lock and undressed. She woke up and ran away from him. The other people in the yard ordered her to go away. The man pulled her until they got to his place. He hit her until she gave in. He raped her two times.

She went to the police and later to the hospital. The medical report showed evidence of 'extra-genital violence'. Later the police could not find the complainant at her place of residence or at the Gaborone Station where she sold fruits. She had absconded and left Gaborone for her home village in Jakalas No 1 in the North East District. The case was closed.

Cases of the nature profiled by Case study 8 mainly applied where the victim had an established intimate relationship with the accused. Often, it was usually an older relative of the victim who would find out that the two were having a sexual relationship. The parents or guardian would then report this incidence to the police and press defilement charges. Sometimes, evidence would show that the victim had been coerced or even beaten by the parents to report her boyfriend to the police and press for the charge of rape. The reluctance of the victim to implicate her lover would prompt her to drop the charges against him or to withdraw the case or abscond.

In certain instances the police may have solid cases that they would like to pursue. But the absence of constructive measures which limit an involved party's ability to withdraw a case, as and when they see fit, forces them to close the case once the said party has decided to drop the charges and withdraw a case. The result is, therefore, that the person who defiled the minor gets away with this crime.

In other cases police fail to prosecute when they are convinced by the perpetrators who claim to have given the girls money and/or beer in return for sex. The girls are said to later renege on the arrangement and the men force them to have sex with them. Though clearly it is unconsented sex, these cases reveal that such girls do set themselves up for danger, sometimes. The case following is illustrative.

Case study 9: Dikeledi
Dikeledi, a 16-year-old girl, went to a shopping complex near where she stayed. Shesaid she met an 'unknown man' who asked her if she knew where a certain 'City' stayed. According to her, the man took her to his room and slapped her on her cheek. He then commanded her to sleep with him. She said she lay down and had sex with him outside the yard and all the time he was saying, '*Basetsana ba malatsi ano ba rata go tshamekisa batho. O bona gore o ka njela madi ke bo*

ke sa robale le wena', meaning, 'Girls of today you like playing around with people. Do you think you can spend my money and then refuse to sleep with me'. The accused claimed that they had agreed to have sex in return for money and beer but after taking his money and his beer she reneged and did not fulfil her part of the deal.

The police concluded that the complainant had given false information and closed the case.

According to the police, sometimes a man and a girl agree on a particular amount per round. When the man fails to pay up or to pay in full, the girl reports the matter as rape. Having established, in their view, that it was consented sex, even when the girl was a minor, and that the problem was that the man had failed to pay as per agreement, some of the police officers advise the girl to sue for *sekoloto* (or payment of debt). We must emphasise, however, that much as this conduct must be condemned, the bottom line is that once a person indicates unwillingness to engage in sex, his or her position must be respected irrespective of whether or not at some stage consent was given. This is so because anyone has a right to withdraw consent at any time and once consent has been withdrawn then any sexual activity thereafter is unlawful and criminal. Moreover, consent to sexual activity by a minor is irrelevant.

6.2 Knowledge and Views about Defilement

Knowledge about the legal definition of defilement, procedures for seeking legal remedies and penalties for such offences varied depending on the professions of the informants. Data was collected from students, police, doctors, traditional leaders and magistrates through group discussions and workshops.

6.2.1 Students

As discussed in the methodology chapter, a brainstorming technique was employed as a strategy to find out the understanding by secondary school students of the concept of defilement without interrupting their thought processes or influencing their responses. The bulk of junior secondary school students neither understood the term 'defilement' nor had they ever heard of it. Even after much probing by the researchers they seemed quite lost. It is only after considerable explanation from the researchers that they admitted to knowing what it was. On the contrary, most of the senior school students had heard of the term defilement before; from their teachers and from the broadcast and print media.

The students offered their definitions of the term defilement. The following are some of the definitions obtained from the students:

- deliberate damage to something;
- to make impure – to dirty;
- something done in a wrong way;
- to do wrong intentionally;
- something done illegally; and
- doing things that one is not allowed to do.

They also expressed their concern about the various contradictions in the law particularly regarding the different age limits specified by different laws. More specifically, they were concerned about the contradictions existing between the law governing defilement and the Marriage Act. While the former defines defilement as the act of having 'unlawful carnal knowledge of any person under the age of 16', the latter sets the marriageable age at 14 and 16 years for girls and boys respectively. As such, the Marriage Act can be utilised to nullify the application of the law on defilement by assuming or even forcing the existence of a marital relationship as a cover up.

The students suggested that the marriageable age should be increased to 21 years because this is the age at which one is legally considered to be an adult in Botswana. They felt that marriageable age of 16 years was too low and the person involved was not 'mature enough.' It also fell within the schoolgoing age and thus hindered the academic pursuits of those affected. According to them, most 16-year-olds are still dependent fully on their parents and guardians for the provision of their needs and also need to 'explore' and expand their horizons before they can settle down to married life. On the strength of the above grounds the students suggested that parents should not be given the right by law to consent to the marriage of an under-age child because in most cases they do so for financial gains.

Most expressed concern about the major role parents played when it came to deciding whether or not their child, a minor, could get married. They argued that leaving the final decision (signing the consent form) to the parents or guardians of the minor only created opportunities for parents or guardians to use their powers to exploit their children. To illustrate, in one of the schools, the students cited the case of a girl forced to marry someone she did not wish to marry simply because the parents liked him or they had received financial assistance from him. They called for an amendment to the law to curtail such parental/guardian powers that culminate in what amounts to forced marriages.

It would make sense to harmonise laws dealing with who is a child so that ultimately there is a fixed age, in terms of which anyone falling below that age is regarded as a child. This can be achieved by adopting the age limit presented by the Convention on the Rights of the Child discussed earlier.

6.2.2 Police Officers
Although the distinction between rape and defilement is clear in the Penal Code, the police have varying ideas on deciding which case is rape and which is defilement. Evidence emerging from group discussions held with police officers revealed only one police station in which police officers were quite familiar with the law and procedures for handling cases of rape and defilement. Overall, the practice varied across police stations with stations utilising varied criteria for categorising cases of sexual abuse. In a majority of the cases it was not clear what basis was used to determine whether a reported case was defilement and not rape and vice versa. For instance, in some police stations, cases where a blood relation of the victim, besides those listed in the Penal Code under the incest law, had violated her sexually would pass as rape and not defilement even when the victim's age was below 16 years.

In one police station the officers were not even aware of the provisions of the Penal Code (Amendment) Act No. 5 of 1998, which deals with rape, defilement and incest. Of particular interest was the suggestion that two police officers in this station had to offer with respect to the cut off age for cases of defilement. According to them the age should be lowered from the current 16 to 12 years because some of the kids 'these days look much older than their ages, and so one was bound to mistake them for being older'. Furthermore, they added, 'nobody asks for another's age and no one volunteers such information'. They also tended to absolve the perpetrators of their irresponsibility saying that *'Monna wa Modimo o ne a sa bone gore golo mo ke ngwana o iponela mosadi'*, literally meaning, 'The man of God [poor man] did not realise that this was a child, he saw a woman'.

6.2.3 Tribal Leaders and Administrators
Similar to offences of incest, cases of defilement do not fall within the jurisdiction of tribal leaders and administrators. Such types of cases are prosecuted at general law courts. The study, however, examined *tshenyo* customary court records and sought the opinions of tribal leaders and administrators concerning such cases. *Tshenyo* is a customary law offence referring to impregnating a woman before she is married, irrespective of her age. Consent is irrelevant. The purpose of the examination of customary courts records dealing with cases of *tshenyo* was to find out if any such cases involved girls below the age of six-

teen. The discussions with tribal leaders focused on the existing laws dealing with rape, incest and defilement, the handling of such offences through traditional customs, and the procedures and punitive measures available at the *kgotla*.

The researchers reviewed *tshenyo* cases for the period 1994 to 1999 for those girls who were below 17 years at the time the offence was committed. The findings revealed that most of the girls were 15 years old and the men they were involved with were between the ages of 20 and 27 years. The age difference between the victim and the perpetrator was thus quite large. The cases were brought before the tribal authorities so that the woman or her family could be compensated, especially in instances where children were born as a result of the union between the girl and the man who impregnated her (the accused).

Based on accounts provided by tribal leaders and administrators, defilement was rare in the olden days. They claimed that no one slept with young girls. Although an elderly man could ask for the hand of a young girl in marriage, he had to wait for her to mature and she did not leave her parental abode before this period of maturity was reached. In addition, the couple did not come into physical contact with each other despite being betrothed. This was according to *setso sa bogologolo*, or the cultural practice of the past.

According to the opinions of the tribal leaders and administrators, the maximum age for defilement should be increased from 16 to 18 years because minors aged 16 years and below *ga ba na boikarabelo*. That is, they do not have the capacity to act in their best interests and take total responsibility for their actions.

Concerning the issue of the existing contradictions between the maximum age (16 years) for defilement and marriageable age of 14 years for girls, the tribal leaders and administrators suggested that a uniform age of 18 years should be adopted for both and applied to both boys and girls. According to them, there were numerous physical complications and dangers posed to a young child who indulged in, or was involuntarily involved in, sexual activities. They were mainly concerned about the HIV pandemic that is commonly spread through sexual encounters and is now claiming many lives.

6.2.4 Magistrates and Doctors

The magistrates who were interviewed for this study made it clear that the position of the law when it came to matters of a sexual nature was that females could not be trusted to tell the truth. As such, magistrates must caution themselves about this fact before they proceed with such matters. This was a reiteration of the magistrates' position during the first stage of the study when they explained that,

☞ the requirement of corroboration is almost always impossible because in the first place law assumes that women were mischievous and unreliable in matters sexual in nature;
☞ the law took as a starting point, that the woman had no credibility and therefore had to prove that she was credible; and that
☞ the evidence of complainants in rape and defilement was treated with suspicion and the standard of proof was very high (WLSA, 1999:131)

The doctors revealed that they were not clear about their role in relation to evidence gathering for the police when it came to sexual offences. They seemed to believe that they were required to give an opinion on whether or not a sexual offence had taken place. According to the magistrates, the doctors were supposed to examine the victim and record their findings only. The opinion sought on the police sexual assault form B.P.73 required medical opinion and not legal opinion such as 'fresh rape', 'no evidence of rape', 'she claims to have been raped'.

Many doctors' medical opinions reflect their ignorance regarding medical evidence required for successful prosecution of sexual offences as they tend to dwell on the presence or absence of spermatozoa in the victim's vagina. Magistrates explained that perhaps doctors were not aware that, legally, a conviction could be obtained without the presence of spermatozoa in the victim's vagina. Therefore, where there were no spermatozoa found, the statement by doctors that 'no spermatozoa found' amounted to verbiage. It is not always that the doctor can tell whether there has been penetration because even with the slightest penetration a conviction can be obtained, and also sometimes the vagina may be naturally lax, or the perpetrator unendowed. Sometimes the perpetrator may have used a condom and in that event there would be no spermatozoa in the vagina.

Both the magistrates and doctors were of the view that some information sought in the police medical form B.P.73 was irrelevant as evidence to secure a conviction. They recommended that the form be amended.

6.3 Victims and Perpetrators of Defilement

The findings of the study showed that young girls were generally the most vulnerable to defilement. The average age of the victims was 13 years with some of the reported cases falling below the age of seven years. The perpetrators varied in age though the majority of them were between the ages of 20 and

30 years.

Table 3 below summarises the relationships between the perpetrator and victims of defilement as revealed from police records. Based on the table, most of the victims knew the perpetrators. The perpetrators were usually acquainted with the victim, friends with the victim, known to the family and, in some cases, were resident in the same neighbourhood as the victim. In one case, a 10-year-old girl, who often visited her friend, had been repeatedly abused by her friend's relative. The man would give her money in return. There was also the case of a 12-year-old girl who had been repeatedly abused by a 23-year-old tenant. Her teacher discovered this when the little girl was six months pregnant. There were few cases of offences taking place between complete strangers compared to offences perpetrated by people the victims knew. Out of the 254 cases reported for both greater Gaborone and greater Francistown, only 74 were by strangers, pointing to the fact that children are more at risk with people they know and trust than with strangers.

TABLE 3: RELATIONSHIPS BETWEEN PERPETRATORS AND VICTIMS OF DEFILEMENT

Relationship	Greater Gaborone	Greater Francistown	Total
Relative	22	7	29
Friend	20	24	44
Neighbour	20	18	38
Acquaintance	30	39	69
Stranger	40	34	74
Total	**132**	**122**	**254**

The study showed that both the victim and the perpetrator usually came from the same tribe, and resided in the same ward. Most of the cases took place within these very same wards. In cases where the accused was not of the same tribe as the victim, he was known to the victim.

The findings of our study revealed a disturbing submissiveness of girl-children to male sexual advances and the abuse is, more often than not, cloaked by the perpetrators in the name of love. The responses of the girl-children to such sexual advances by, particularly, adult males to whom they are related or those community members known to them and their families, indicate their confusion and or dilemma. As indicated in the previous chapter, children are generally socialised not to show disrespect for their elders. Society, however, fails to equip them with appropriate skills to protect themselves from or challenge sexual advances by their elders. Hence they tend to helplessly surrender to such demands.

6.4 Places Where Defilement Is Committed

The findings of our study revealed that the offence of defilement is committed mostly within the home, close to the home and with people who know each other. Sometimes, however, the crime is committed outside the home in places such as a nearby bush, on the way home from a nightclub or from night church prayers. The incidences took place at any time of the day although in many cases young girls were defiled during the day while older children were victimised at dusk or at night. Table 4 depicts the kinds of places where the crime of defilement was committed as indicated in police records.

TABLE 4: PLACES WHERE OFFENCES OF DEFILEMENT WERE COMMITTED – BY STUDY AREA

Place	Greater Gaborone	Greater Francistown	Total
Home	34	15	49
Bush	10	6	16
School	2	1	3
Church	2	1	3
Bars/nightclubs	12	11	23
Not specified	72	88	160
Total	**132**	**122**	**254**

Based on the table it is clear that there is no safe place for children as the offence of defilement occurs almost anywhere including within the home, which is supposed to be the safest place. Presented below are illustrative descriptions of what actually happens at the various places.

6.4.1 Home

Contrary to expectations, there is strong suggestion that most of the time the offences of defilement are committed within the home of either the perpetrator or the victim.

As the table shows, the unspecified locations where offences of defilement occurred far outnumber other locations put together. It is clear, however, that police officers are not at all consistent in their documentation, not specifying 63% of the locations of defilement. Despite this, among the locations specified in police reports, the majority of the offences of defilement (52%) occurred either in the home of the perpetrator or of the victim.

The case study presented below illustrates how the perpetrator convinced the victim to go with him to his house.

Case study 10: Legae
An 8-year-old girl was going to school in the morning, when a 17-year-old boy, Legae, called her and asked her to have sex with him. He offered to pay her for it. He asked her where she went to school, and he told her that time was still abundant and that she would not be late for school. She agreed to go with him to his house. He then removed her underwear and had sexual intercourse with her. He, however, says that his penis could not penetrate her vagina and he therefore discontinued sex with her. Then she asked him for the money and he said he did not have any. The girl said she was going to tell her grandmother. He pleaded with her not to, but she insisted.

The study also revealed instances where the mother's boyfriend repeatedly defiled the children and further investigations revealed that the house belonged to the boyfriend who was supporting the family.

The police records also showed that sometimes the crime is committed within the home of the victim. The case of a 17-year-old girl who was raped on two occasions by a boy who stayed on her uncle's plot is illustrative. As mentioned earlier, most such cases end up being withdrawn from the police by complainants or victims because the victims know the perpetrators and they prefer to settle the matter at family level.

6.4.2 The Bush
Defilement sometimes takes place within the vicinity of the home. Case study 11 presented below testifies to this fact.

Case study 11: Berry
A 15-year-old girl went to the bush to look for the goats to bring them back to the homestead before sunset. This was just outside her back yard, not too far away. She saw a wild berry tree, *mogonogono* and stopped to pick some berries. Two men grabbed her from behind and one said, *'O seka wa gadima'*, meaning, 'Do not glance at me'. He took out a penknife and tore her skirt which they used to tie up her arms and to blindfold her. They then dragged her away to some distance from where they had found her. The first man raped her and when he had finished he said, *'ke feditse'* which means 'I am finished'. He suggested that they kill her, but the other man said 'NO!' After he was through with her they took her back to a nearby hill and left her there and ran off. She crawled back to the nearest yard on her knees, sought help and then fainted.

The victim's medical report stated as follows: 'Dirty, smelly, with grass and sand. Painful pelvis. Unable to walk without pain. Appears to be very upset due to forced sexual contact'. The perpetrators were undetected as she could not identify them and a warrant of arrest was issued.

Gang rapes were also widely reported where the victim was often times dragged off the road into the bush and defiled. In one case a 16-year-old girl was gang raped on her way to a kiosk by a 63-year-old man and his friends who alleged that they were escorting her. Our study revealed that some offenders would often entice the victim with sweets, gifts and small amounts of money. The victim would then be lured into the bushes or forced into their own homes or the offenders' and threatened with a knife and death if she refused to grant sexual intercourse.

6.4.3 School Grounds
The study showed that the offence of defilement was not limited to the home and the bush. Young girls were often defiled within school grounds and at public places such as bars and shebeens. Case study 12 is an example of defilement that occurred within school grounds.

Case study 12: Panda
A 16-year-old girl was walking to school when she met a classmate. As they walked together to school, he asked her to go with him to 'Panda', a bushy spot

along the school fence used by late comers to jump into the schoolyard without being seen by the teachers. They arrived at Panda at about seven a.m. It was her first time at Panda. She told the boy that she wanted to go through the main gate because the fence was too high. The boy said to her 'zama style, give me the style', then he tripped her, took off her panties and raped her. The two missed registration and the first two lessons of school that day.

6.4.4 Other Places
In another case a seven-year-old girl was picked up by an unknown man at the school gate where she was waiting for a taxi to take her home. The girl resisted but the man forced her into his car and took her to an unoccupied house. He took the girl's panties off and when the child screamed he stopped, picked her up and ran to a nearby bush. Before he could reach the bush, he saw a police car, dropped the child and ran away.

6.5 Factors Contributing to Defilement
The study revealed that various factors contributed to the offence of defilement such as shared accommodation, poor parenting and early marriages.

6.5.1 Shared Accommodation
The issue of shared accommodation in poor families has proven to be one of the factors facilitating defilement. Male relatives, friends and visitors often end up sharing a room or hut with young children due to lack of adequate space. This renders the girl-child susceptible to sexual abuse. In one of the cases examined, a 15-year-old girl was sexually abused by her brother's housemate while his brother was sleeping in his own room. Though the perpetrator admitted having sexual intercourse with the girl, the case was dismissed as not having sufficient evidence because the girl did not cry out for help.

A newspaper article also reported a case of that nature. The article read thus: 'In Palapye, 45-year-old Otshidile Ranto Tshenyego has been sentenced to 10 years imprisonment for defilement of a 10 year-old girl. Tshenyego raped the 10-year-old who was sharing a hut with him and other children. Seven people, including the child's father testified against the accused.' *(Mmegi/The Reporter,* 22–28 March 1996:8)

6.5.2 Poor Parenting
The issue of poor parenting was also raised, particularly by youn people. They

asserted that a lot of children grew up with bad parenting. Many parents did not take full responsibility of being parents. Some parents prefer it when their daughters bring home a working 'son-in-law' and the so called sons-in-law were often older men who were working, and who subsequently defiled these young girls. In addition, some adults often practised absentee parenthood. For example, in one case a young single mother with teenage children went away for days on end visiting a boyfriend. When she got back home she discovered that her 14-year-old daughter had also been away from home for the same amount of days she had been away. She went to the police to report that her daughter had been defiled.

In another case, a 14-year-old community junior secondary school student was coming from a nightclub at around six in the morning when a man accosted her. The man started harassing her and pulling her off the road. The girl was saved by the public who came out of their houses, ran after the suspect, caught up with him and handed him to the police. The case was later closed because of lack of evidence as the complainant was playing truant, stopped going to school altogether and absconded. In yet another case involving a community junior secondary school student, a 15-year-old girl was gang raped by six young men after they had picked her up from a nightclub. This incident occurred at around three in the morning.

Those interviewed for the study also felt that where parents were not working, girl-children were forced to have sex for money. Some children are abused by neighbours because of lack of certain amenities in their households such as television, which pushes them into the neighbour's house. Nevertheless, according to the students, if there had been more parental responsibility and guidance such things could have been avoided despite the poverty.

6.5.3 Early Marriages

The Marriage Act, Section 17, states that 'no minor or person below the age of 21 years, not being a widow or widower, may marry without the consent, in writing of his or her parents or guardian'. Many men, who end up having sexual relations with minor children, have exploited this law. Usually they enter into 'traditional agreements' with the girls' parents, where they promise to marry the girls or where they provide monetary rewards. After a while, they change their minds and abandon the girls. Secondary school students shared with the research team situations where their schoolmates were forced to leave school to enter into marriages arranged by parents. The following newspaper article published in the *Midweek Sun*, 22 July 1998:3) is illustrative:

A 27-year-old man is accused of sexually abusing a 13-year-old girl in Tutume village. Police said that the unemployed man has had an affair with the girl since she was 12 years old. He is alleged to have made a traditional agreement with the minor's parents to marry her in future, but apparently he changed his mind recently and broke up the relationship. The couple has been seeing each other on a regular basis, with the would-be husband sometimes taking the girl to stay at his place for days. Police said the girl who does not attend school was found to be suffering from a venereal disease...

6.5.4 Unwillingness to Report Defilement Cases
Most people are unwilling to report offences of a sexual nature because of the stigma attached to them and this situation only serves to perpetuate the crime. The offences occur daily, yet the number of cases reported still remains low. This low rate of reportage can be explained as follows:

- the victim's fear of the perpetrator, especially in cases where he has threatened to harm them if they report.
- the victim's fear of not being believed by their parents or the police.
- the victim's fear of being stigmatised. The victim already carries feelings of shame, guilt and low self-esteem. Hence they do not want to make themselves more vulnerable by revealing the crime.

In one case, the victim did not report the incident until she was assaulted again by another student. According to the *Botswana Gazette* (15 July 1998:3):

A 16-year-old female student at Tonota Community Junior Secondary School has been allegedly raped by school colleagues. The Station Commander Mojakgomo said the girl reported that she was raped the first of this month, but she did not tell anyone. A few days after the incident, she was assaulted by another student and shortly was found crying by a teacher who found out from the girl that she had been raped and reported the incident to the police.

In another case, other victims of defilement committed by the same perpetrator emerged only when one victim got the courage to report the incident. The case involved a 30-year-old male teacher at Maboane Primary School in Kweneng District who was arrested for molesting male students aged 13 to 15 years. As the station commander, Superintendent Sonny Kula, indicated, 'Our investigations have so far proved that several such incidents have taken place as nine other male students have come forward with the same story of being molested by the accused teacher' *(Botswana Guardian*, 9 August 1996:1). According to the station commander, the students told the police that they had been molested continuously since last year, but were too frightened to disclose anything.

The examples above clearly show that stigmatization of the crime against the victim instead of the perpetrator contributes to further victimization of the victim and gives the perpetrators more courage to continue committing the crime since they know they will not be punished for their actions as nobody will tell. Speaking out, however, exposes the criminals and gives other victims courage to speak out as well.

Family members, usually the parents of the victim, may opt not to report the incident. Often, in a case where the perpetrator is known, the parents may opt to settle the issue out of court. The perpetrator is asked to pay a fine to the family or if the victim is pregnant, then he is asked to pay either *tshenyo* (seduction damages), or maintenance for the child instead of going to prison for defilement. This is seen as a way of handling the sensitive matter as quietly and as quickly as possible without involving a third and fourth party – usually the police, magistrates and social workers. However, previous WLSA (1992) research has shown that in most cases, payment for seduction or maintenance is never made. Thus, more often than not, perpetrators go unpunished and this may encourage repeated offences.

CONSEQUENCES OF INCEST AND DEFILEMENT

The offences of incest and defilement have negative consequences on the survivor and even the family of the survivor as a whole. The consequences can be in the form of physical injuries, psychological and mental trauma, financial loss or a combination of any of the above.

7.1 Effects on Children

Experts agree that children who are victims of sexual abuse are generally negatively affected. Clearly their self-esteem is severely damaged. The fundamental problem with adult-child abuse is the violation by the adult of a child's trust. Sexual abuse is a devastating experience for most children. Very few of the children escape with no apparent ill effects. For the majority of them there are two common effects. The first involves the suppression of feeling, coolness in relationships with persons of both sexes, withdrawal, and trouble relating to peers. The other typical response is to become self-destructive.

7.1.1 Sexually Transmitted Diseases

Many children contract sexually transmitted diseases from the offences of incest and defilement committed against them. Such effects on children are clearly illustrated in Case study 1 (see Chapter 5). The mother of five visited the WLSA offices seeking help to rescue her girl-children from their abusive father. According to her, one time during school holidays, her eight-year-old and 17-year-old daughters visited her. She realised that the younger girl was walking in a strange way, *a nanabela*. When she investigated she noticed that the girl's panties had some discharge on them. She took both her daughters to a doctor who examined them. The mother had copies of the doctor's records of her findings, which revealed that both girls had relaxed genital muscles and were infected with sexually transmitted diseases.

In another case, an eight-year-old girl was referred to an NGO by a doctor at the Princess Marina Hospital. The girl had been admitted to Princess Marina with chronic syphilis. This child's parents were Basarwa (San) who worked as cattle post (farm) help on a 'Motswana's' cattle post. The three people who came to the hospital showing the same symptoms were the eight-year-old girl, the farm owner (a man) and the wife of the farm owner.

For obvious reasons the HIV status of any of the above could not be disclosed to the researchers. However, in a country where the rate of HIV/AIDS is recorded as one of the highest in the world, it cannot be ruled out that some, if not all, of the parties involved may have been infected.

7.1.2 Psychological Trauma

Children undergo psychological trauma, which clearly manifests itself in their behavioural changes. An examination of records at one of the NGOs revealed that victims of incest or defilement portrayed unusual behaviour. They often played truant, stole, lied or simply ran away from home. One thirteen-year-old girl wrote school essays depicting sexual activities, and when counselled by social workers it was discovered that her father had been sexually abusing her and her siblings repeatedly.

Case study 1 provides a good illustration of the trauma experienced by children as a result of incest. To recall: as related by the mother, one of her daughters, the 13-year-old, informed her that she had refused to continue having sexual intercourse with her father and wanted to live with her mother. Her father later disowned her. She became depressed and received psychological treatment and counselling. She lost her concentration and her grades dropped at school. When interviewed by the court to find out why she preferred to live with her mother, the girl clammed up and would not reveal what she had earlier revealed to the mother. The 17-year-old profiled in the same case study eventually got to a point where she could not take any more of what her father was doing to her. One night she did not go to her father's bed. Instead she sneaked her boyfriend into the house. When her father discovered this he gave the two a good beating. The girl later thought of drinking rat poison but later decided against it and used a rope instead. When the rope became painful she tried to pull it off to stop it from going in any deeper. She ended up scratching herself severely on the neck. The domestic helper came to her rescue and cut the rope. The only son in the family, a university graduate, has been so affected that he has divorced himself totally from the rest of the family. He lives alone and does not visit the home of either his mother or his father.

7.1.3 Promiscuity

Some victims of incest and defilement respond to the experience by becoming sexually promiscuous. This is illustrated by a case that was examined in one of the NGOs studied. It involved a 15-year-old girl who had played truant for a whole week. Her father, a police officer, went looking for her and finally found her. She revealed that during that week she had had sexual intercourse with four different men: a teacher, a priest, an ex-boyfriend, and a current boyfriend. At the time her father found her she was with her current boyfriend drinking at a bar in one of the villages. The girl's file further revealed that a bus driver had raped her on a school trip the previous year. The bus driver was convicted but no help was offered to the traumatised victim. As a result her self-esteem was eroded and she engaged in this type of behaviour.

7.1.4 Senses of Resentment, Anger and Self-doubt

Victims of incest and defilement also display a sense of resentment, anger and self-doubt. This was clearly evident from the victim profiled in Case studies 1 and 2 presented in Chapter Five. In Case study 1, the father of the victims profiled once took one of the daughters shopping. On their arrival back home from shopping, he asked her to show the sisters the clothes he had bought her. He there and then, in the presence of the sisters, gave the girl P100. The sisters became jealous of such special treatment given to their sister and one of the girls informed the mother, wondering where they had gone wrong. In Case study 2, on the other hand, Dawn was put in a place of safety while awaiting her father's trial. Her siblings often phoned her and accused her of causing problems in the family. They said, 'Right now you are there in that place eating three meals a day. You have caused papa to stop buying us food and clothes because you have spoken about this thing'.

7.2 Effects on Mothers

The immediate reaction of mothers of abused children is somewhat similar: disbelief and denial. Subsequent reactions vary depending on the circumstances the woman finds herself in. To illustrate, in the example profiled by Case study 1 in Chapter 5, the mother of the victim explained that she had had suspicions that her husband was sexually abusing their children even before their divorce, but she had had no proof. Her children had told her, even then, that when she was away in town and they were in the village with their father, the father would ask them to share his bed. When she divorced him, she had hoped that she would get custody of the children and rescue them from him. However, she did not bring up the issue of incest in her divorce case as ground to secure custody. Afterwards when she tried to appeal for the custody of the children it was then that she brought out the issue of incest. None of the children spoke out before a judge in court and there were no grounds upon which the judge could reverse the court's decision.

The victim's mother later took the matter to the tribal authorities who, according to her, mocked her in court for behaving in such an unacceptable manner of revealing intimate family matters. She was even labelled mentally unstable. She confessed that indeed she suffered from mental depression as a result of the suffering her children were going through. She underwent electro-convulsive-therapy, was on anti-depressants, suffered from anaemia, and was unable to eat, saying, *'Ke nna ke kgotshe kutlobotlhoko'*, that is, 'I am always full of suffering, and I am unable to eat'. She further explained that she was so disturbed by this whole thing that at work she was irritable and insubordinate and her boss had once threatened to beat her up.

The study also revealed that in some cases of abuse of children by their stepfathers or their mothers' boyfriends, the mothers blame the offence on the abused girl. They claim that the girl enticed the man. In addition, it was found that some mothers of abused children found it hard to discuss the issue even with authorities. The situation was even worse when they had a relationship with the perpetrator. This is evident in the example presented under Case study 3 in Chapter 5. To recap: it involved a daughter who was being abused by her stepfather and was reluctant to go home for holidays. Both her parents wanted her to go to their home during the holidays. When questioned by the authorities the victim's mother had the following to say: 'I am an adult woman. I've been with many men and this is the only one who wanted to marry me. So, I want the girl back home'. This kind of response from a mother, particularly since she was not interviewed for her side of the story, may be interpreted as a reflection of her condoning of the abusive relationship so as to save her marriage. The researchers did not get the opportunity to interview either the girl or the mother. The authorities could not reveal the identities of the parties involved. They could only hint that the perpetrator was someone too high up in the hierarchies of power and they could not reveal his identity for fear of losing their jobs. Had this case been brought out into the open, it would have been one of very best cases to use to lobby for the inclusion of stepfathers in those sections of the Penal Code dealing with incest in Botswana. As it is, when it comes to this practice, secrecy abounds at all levels of society. Incest by nature questions the integrity of the family, the very cornerstone of society.

In most of the cases the mothers of the children who are abused by their fathers and stepfathers find themselves in a situation where they are not able to offer help or support to their children, even in cases where their children have approached them for help. This could be attributed to the mother's determination to sustain her relationship even if it means sacrificing the child's wellbeing. The case of a 17-year-old girl who was being sexually abused by two of her paternal uncles is illustrative. She eventually appealed to her father. However, in the process of narrating her problems to her father, the father started caressing her instead of addressing the concerns she had about his abusive brothers. She later informed her mother of her ordeal but the mother, she asserted, totally ignored her. The victim then decided to seek help from an NGO dealing with issues of domestic violence. The officers from the organization eventually spoke to the mother and she admitted that the daughter had sought her help. She did not deny that the men in the family were molesting her daughter. The counsellors at the NGO explained that the woman did not show any emotion. She was like a blank wall.

7. 3 Effects on Fathers

Some of the perpetrators who sexually abuse their children sometimes find it very difficult to deal with the problem when they are eventually discovered and have to face the wrath of the law. Some may even contemplate or actually commit suicide. Indeed, based on the findings of this study, two fathers and an uncle committed suicide when they were found to have committed the crimes of incest and the matters reported to the police. More specifically, in Case study 2, when Dawn's father was eventually arrested, he committed suicide in police custody. The family blamed Dawn for the suicide.

PROCEDURES FOR HANDLING INCEST AND DEFILEMENT CASES

The examination of police records and discussions with the police revealed procedures they employ in handling cases of sexual assault in Botswana. The steps in the procedure included recording of statements, investigation, arrest, issuance of warrant of arrest, prosecution, case withdrawals, negotiation and reconciliation, use of medical form B.P.73, and the step-by-step recording of the progress of the case in the investigation diary.

8.1 Recording Statements

Once a case of incest or defilement is reported to the police, the first step taken is for the police to record a statement from the complainant. Based on information extracted from police records, police officers were often not sensitive to the experiences of the victims when they recorded their statements. Narratives from different victims revealed that victims suffered various ordeals at the hands of the recording officers. The procedure utilised to record the statement gave the impression that the victims all went through the same experience. The use of language in the statements was also perplexing in that when the officer recorded a statement from a girl-child aged seven years, it would read the same way as that received from a 42-year-old woman. For instance, the statements from both victims would read, 'The rapist took off my panty, he inserted his penis inside my vagina, he moved up and down until he ejaculated, and a white substance came out'.

It is disturbing to imagine that a seven-year-old child could possibly posses such vocabulary to describe a sexual act. In fact, it is highly unlikely that such a child would even know about ejaculation and sperm. In such a case, therefore, it is possible that the police put words into her statement. Police officers also appeared to use unintelligible language. For example, we came across the term 'condundrumming' several times in the records, and when we asked some officers what the word meant no one seemed to know. On the contrary NGOs addressing such matters report the statements in the language of the victim. A five-year-old girl, for example, explained to her grandmother that *'Malome o ne a ntira dilo tse di maswe. O ne a nnyoka'*. That is, 'My (maternal) uncle was doing bad things to me. He was having sex with me'. *Nnyoka* is a childish word to describe the sexual act.

8.2 The Medical Report

For sexual abuse to be prosecuted successfully it is necessary that the victim undergoes a medical examination. A medical doctor must attend to the victim and examine her or him for any signs of injuries sustained, or whether sexual intercourse actually took place. The results of the examination are recorded in a police medical form B.P.73. This form is part of the investigation diary and should be attached to the docket. Details entered in such forms are quite scanty and leave one to speculate whether or not sexual intercourse had occurred. In other words, the information is open to misinterpretation. The general conclusion presented by most forms examined was as follows: 'Alleged rape' or 'Difficult to conclude because complainant is sexually active'. To say the least, the form is inadequate and unclear as to what criteria is used to suggest that a victim had been raped. This calls for some rethinking of its structure and format.

The above position was supported by data gathered from an interview with a medical doctor who expressed the concern about the structure and format of the police form B.P.73. In his own words, the form was 'only trying to pick up the extreme forms of rape, as it only looked for the physical signs which may suggest that the offence took place'. These included signs such as scratches and bruises on the body or genitalia. Yet, the definition of rape involved 'other aspects other than the physical conditions'. The doctor explained that 'for instance, the absence of a hymen did not necessarily mean that rape had occurred as the hymen could be broken even during activities such as horse riding and other physically strenuous occupations'. The doctor also indicated that having to insert a certain number of fingers into a female victim's genitals was degrading and that the process itself could not determine whether or not the victim had been raped. In addition, the medical form B.P.73 has a section which asks whether a victim was sexually active. This seems to infer that the mere fact that a person was sexually active reduced the probability that she had been raped. Thus, other than subjecting women to inhuman and degrading treatment, form B.P.73 is no longer relevant because the definition of rape has been changed with the result that vaginal penetration by a penis is not necessarily a relevant element.

8.3 Manner of Investigation

An examination of the investigation diary kept by police revealed that police officers do a lot of work in following up their cases. They record every action they take in the investigation process. This might include making sure that the complainant goes for the medical examination, following up the complainant and looking for the accused who more often than not absconds. There was also evidence of regular and sustained communication between the investigating officer and his seniors right up to the officer commanding the Station.

The investigating officers use a method of investigation called confrontation, which includes bringing together the victim and the suspect in order that they can relate their sides of the story to see who of the two will succumb to pressure. In confronting sexual offences the police take both the complainant and the suspect to the scene of the crime. At the scene they look for struggle marks, shoe marks and trampled grass, among others. But in sexual offences, which are traumatic in nature, the approach is usually detrimental to the woman or the girl because it forces her to relive the whole sordid affair thus traumatising her further. The approach also creates conditions that facilitate suspects to play on the sympathy of the complainants or to threaten them further. This, combined with the trauma suffered by the victims, is responsible for the withdrawal of many rape, incest or defilement cases by complainants.

This investigative procedure does not take into account the victim's rights at all. To illustrate, in Mochudi a 17-year-old boy raped an eight-year-old girl on her way to school. In the investigating diary the police officer wrote:

> I confronted both the complainant and the suspect. The complainant identified the suspect to be the one who raped her. The victim, a standard II pupil at Isang Primary School aged 8 years of Mosanta ward Mochudi, was taken to (DRM) Deborah Retief Memorial Hospital where she was examined by a qualified doctor. The scene was later visited after her discharge from hospital. This was done in the presence of the accused and the victim, also in the presence of the elder sister of the accused.

The detective constable to whom the investigating officer was reporting had the following remarks to make: 'Take the accused person to social welfare offices. He must be accompanied by one of the close relatives who know his background because his mother has passed away'. There was no mention of, or concern over, the eight-year-old victim whatsoever.

8.4 Arrest and Warrant of Arrest

The procedure followed when a crime has been committed is that, upon notification, the police look for the suspect to make an arrest. A significant number of cases, however, are closed because the perpetrators are not found. This is common in cases of rape, including defilement involving strangers. The following case study is illustrative.

Case study 13: Cressida
A 15-year-old girl went from Gaborone to Mochudi where her parents had sent her. Afterwards she went to the traditional choirs with her sister. At 6 p.m. her 19-year-old sister got her a lift back to Gaborone from a Toyota Cressida taxi. She took down the registration number. The taxi man picked up a woman whom he went to drop off in Rasesa, a neighbouring village. After dropping off the woman, who was the sister to the taxi driver, he proposed love to the girl and she refused. He then went off the tarred road and drove to some deserted fields where, it is written in her statement, 'He intercoursed me four times'.

The taxi driver dropped the girl off at Taung bus stop in Gaborone at 00:30 hours and gave her P10.00. Because her mother was away at a funeral in Shoshong, the girl informed her neighbours about what happened. The neighbours went with her to the police station. Instead of taking her to hospital first for examination, the police decided to take her to the home of the woman who was dropped off at Rasesa. The woman confirmed that she had indeed seen the little girl in the car when her brother had gone to drop her off and she further said she did not notice if there was any relationship between her brother and the little girl in the car. After spending three hours at the taxi rank looking for the suspect without success, the police decided that the accused was at large and they issued a warrant of arrest.

There are two questions that emanate from the above case study. First, why did the police not take the girl to hospital first for medical examination before visiting the female passenger who had been dropped off by the taxi driver before he raped her, yet a medical report is an important element in the prosecution docket? Second, after looking for the suspect for three hours unsuccessfully, why did they hurriedly declare the suspect was at large and issue a warrant of arrest before exhausting all possible leads? The answers to these questions may hinge on the seriousness with which the police treat cases of rape, incest or defilement. The action of issuing a warrant of arrest by police is common practice in cases where the alleged perpetrator is identified but his whereabouts are not known. Once arrested, the suspect is remanded in custody for 48 hours pending appearance before a judicial officer. It should be noted that in cases where the warrant of arrest is issued by the court, the police proceed to close the file and put it away in a store room. There it may not come off the shelves until a researcher finds it.

When the accused first appears before the magistrate to answer the charges, the magistrate uses his or her discretion to grant him bail upon application. The procedure is that the perpetrator appears for mention, but the law does not require the presence of the victim. This is so because, technically, the complainant is the state, and through the presence of the police prosecutor, the state is therefore present. The victim, being a key witness is only needed on the day of the trial. What is disturbing, however, is the fact that such bail is often granted without taking into consideration the peril of the victim, who might be in danger of continued violation, or threats or obstruction of justice. The magistrate sets a date for the next appearance. If the accused does not turn up without good reason, suggesting that he has not complied with the conditions of the bail, the court may issue a warrant for his arrest.

8.5 The Trial Process

Based on information gathered from magistrate courts, most of the trials did not take long. A few had to be mentioned a number of times due to the involved parties' failure to collect materials required to be presented before the court: the trials generally lasted from a couple of days to a number of weeks.

Prior to the Penal Code (Amendment) Act 1998, there was no minimum sentence for sexual crimes. However, the law provided for a maximum sentence of life imprisonment. Table 5 overleaf shows the sentences for defilement for the period covered by the study, 1994–1999.

As evident from the table, despite the provision for life imprisonment sentence (Penal Code, Chapter 08:01), no maximum sentencing was handed down during the period covered by the study, 1994-999. This sentencing trend raises concerns as to whether judicial officers do not regard the offence of defilement to be sufficiently grave to warrant steep sentences. While acknowledging that magistrates have the discretion on sentencing, it is unacceptable that magistrates should, in the exercise of this discretion, sentence convicts to five to six years for an offence where the maximum is life imprisonment.

The Penal Code, however, has since been amended. According to the Penal Code (Amendment) Act 1998, the penalty for defilement, as for rape, is a mini-

TABLE 5: SENTENCES PASSED ON SEXUAL CRIMES INVOLVING MINORS (1994–1999)

Year	Victim's Age (years)	Offender's Age (years)	Offence Committed	Sentence Passed
1994	14	37	Defilement	5 years
1994	9	32	Defilement	5 years
1994	13	39	Defilement	4 years and 4 strokes
1995	15	19	Attempted Defilement.	5 years – reduced to 3 years, 4 strokes
1996	10	45	Defilement	10 years
1997	16	34	Defilement	10 years
1998	12	38	Defilement	8 years
1998	14	27	Defilement	10 years and 3 strokes

mum of 10 years imprisonment. Where the perpetrator tests HIV-positive the minimum penalty is 15 years imprisonment. This can increase to a minimum of 20 years if the perpetrator had knowledge of being HIV-positive and therefore intentionally spread it to the victim. The penalty for incest, on the other hand, is a maximum of five years imprisonment. No mandatory HIV/AIDS test is required. This begs for the questions: why such leniency when it comes to the crime of incest; does our law condone incest; is sexual abuse of children by their parents and closest relatives, upon whom they look for protection, a lesser crime than defilement and rape?

Notwithstanding the above, some of the magistrates showed concern over the issue of child sexual abuse as evidenced by the following remarks: 'It is obvious that rape entails a series of offences and subjects the victim to all sorts of agony. As noted in the judgement, the poor girl was subjected to mental and physical torture which she would live with the whole of her life'. This was said by a magistrate who was sentencing a convict for eight years for rape instead of defilement of an eight-year-old girl. Another magistrate who was sentencing a 23-year-old man, found guilty of raping an 11-year-old girl, to a period of five years in prison and three strokes of the cane, had the following to say:

The primary concern of the law in such cases is to protect the virginity of girls under the prescribed age. Surely these are young [and] not mature enough to consent to having sexual intercourse. It is very sad and most disquieting that the accused found it proper to have sexual intercourse or have a love affair with such a girl when there are no doubt many girls and women who may have been more than willing to give it to him at no price.

Sometimes a perpetrator is granted bail after citing various reasons the court is satisfied with. This often leads to a situation where the perpetrator then absconds and the legal representatives have to track him down, usually without much success. As a result, the trial cannot proceed in the absence of the accused. The cases are consequently withdrawn with liberty to prosecute and the police can issue a warrant of arrest against him. In other incidences, the cases are withdrawn because a party did not follow the correct procedures or because of the existence of certain inconsistencies in their testimonies which prevent the court from coming to a fair decision.

During group discussion, most of the students, police officers and tribal leaders felt that the five year maximum imprisonment meted for incest was too lenient and should be increased to the same level as that for defilement and rape. According to some students, compared to incest offenders, those who committed the offence of defilement received much stiffer penalties. This occurred despite the fact that in some cases of defilement the victim had wanted to have a sexual relationship with her partner and the two had agreed to be involved in such a relationship. Most students and police officers argued that incest was the worst form of sexual abuse, particularly where the abuser is the biological father. They suggested that its punishment should be life imprisonment. In their view, the current penalty allows perpetrators to be out within five years to pounce on their victims again. The students suggested that, in light of the suffering perpetrators subject victims to, they should undergo a lot of suffering through life imprisonment rather than through hanging which would subject them to a very short period of pain before they are dead. Some informants even suggested measures such as death by stoning and castration in cases such as the one where an eight-year-old was admitted to hospital with chronic syphilis.

A minority of students nevertheless felt that five years was too much. One of the students at a community junior secondary school felt very strongly that she could not bear to live five months without seeing her father, let alone five years. This particular student was quite emotional about the issue. She exclaimed, 'Five years *o sa mmone!* That is too much. *Mama a sala a tlisa banna mo lapeng; mo lapeng go sala go itaolwa'*, meaning that five years without seeing her father was too much and that her mother would then bring other men home with everyone doing as they pleased – being delinquent. According to this student, having sexual intercourse with one's father was 'having an affair' with him. She asserted that in some cases '…the child consented. She knew exactly what she was doing.'

The students in particular felt that the penalty for defilement was 'unfair' and they gave reasons for this. Some stated that it was contrary to the Human Rights Charter, which states that every person has the right to choose what they want to do. Therefore, the law of defilement was interfering with a person's personal choice and decision. They also felt that a minimum penalty of ten years for 'someone who wanted to make love to someone they loved was too much'. Although they were in favour of a law which 'protected someone who is still a child and is innocent', they did not think that the older party (the one who defiled the minor), should be sent to prison because '…they loved each other and they made love to each other'.

SUMMARY AND RECOMMENDATIONS

In this chapter, the key findings of the study are synthesised and various policy recommendations put forth. The basic objective of the policy proposals presented by the study is to create an environment in which the problems of incest and defilement can be dealt with more effectively both at the prevention and prosecution levels.

9.1 Summary of Findings

This study examined the social, cultural and legal factors that perpetuate offences of defilement and incest, two of the most overlooked and under-reported crimes in Botswana. It aimed at providing information, raising awareness, lobbying for policy and law reform and influencing attitudinal changes for purposes of promoting the eradication of violence against women and children in our society. The focus of the study was on the girl-child.

The study findings revealed that there are various definitions of a child both from the customary and general law perspectives. According to Setswana custom, there is no cut-off age for a child. Anybody younger than another person is considered a child by that person. General law, on the other hand, uses age as the basis of defining a child. However, the various statutes have diverse cut-off ages. According to the Interpretation Act (Sec. 49) the legal age of majority is 21 years. At the same time, any person aged 16 years has the legal capacity to consent to sexual intercourse (Penal Code, Cap. 08:01 Sec. 147). Girls and boys aged 14 and 16 years, respectively, may marry with the consent of a guardian (Marriage Act, Cap. 29:01, Sec. 16). Thus, the Marriage Act contradicts the law of defilement which clearly states that it is a crime for any person to have sexual intercourse with a girl or boy under the age of 16 years. The diverse cut-off ages of who is a child among the various laws leave a lot of room for abuse of children. Some men have used the promise of marriage to avoid prosecution for defilement. Furthermore, many Batswana are not aware that having sexual intercourse with a person under the age of 16 years is a criminal offence.

Our study also showed that, although incest is a crime in Botswana, an impenetrable wall of silence nonetheless shelters it. Offences of incest do occur, but for the most part they are kept a family secret. In the rare event that crimes of incest are reported to the police, they often classified it as rape. This conceals the fact that, despite the hard work and long hours police put into seriously pursuing cases of sexual abuse and their determination to prevent them, adults in our society sexually abuse minors. According to the Penal Code (Amendment) Act, 1998, one is said to have committed the offence of incest if he or she has sexual intercourse with another person 'knowing that person to be his or her grandchild, child, brother, sister or parent' (Cap. 08:01 Sec. 147). The Penal Code further includes half brothers and half sisters among those persons prohibited from having sexual intercourse (Cap. 08:01, Sec. 168). Many informants criticised the list of relatives as provided by the Penal Code arguing that it was based on the western concept of the nuclear family. They pointed out that family in Botswana is broader and therefore the list should include uncles, aunts, step-parents and cousins. They particularly singled out maternal uncles as the worst perpetrators of incest. According to the information adduced by the study, this was said to be so because the uncles' sexual abuse of their nieces was concealed behind the Setswana customary practice of *ditlhogo*.

The practice of *ditlhogo* is entrenched by the gender imbalance of power and authority between women and men in the various Setswana customary laws and practices. These leave a lot of room for abuse of women and children. The study found the Setswana customary socialization of children in general and of girl-children in particular to be contributory to the perpetuation of sexual offences against them. It discourages assertiveness, promotes the children's inability to challenge or question male sexual advances, and turns them into partners by keeping such offences against them family secrets. It would be logical to conclude that the fact that Setswana customary practices make it is easy for fathers and (maternal) uncles to sexually exploit daughters and nieces, respectively, increases the probability of the offence of incest occurring in Botswana. Paradoxically, however, whenever victims report such incidences they are rarely believed by other family members or by law enforcement authorities.

The study noted the discrepancy in the penalties between defilement and incest. Whereas the penalty for defilement is a minimum of ten years imprisonment (and HIV testing once one was found guilty), in the case of incest there is no minimum penalty. The law, instead, provides for a maximum of five years imprisonment with no provision for HIV testing. Most informants of the study expressed concern at the leniency of the penalty for incest, asserting that incest was a more serious crime than defilement and therefore deserved a death sentence.

Based on the finding of the study, it may be concluded that for many children, and contrary to expectation, the home is the most dangerous place. It does not provide a safe and secure environment as many of the crimes of defilement and incest are committed within the home by people the children know and trust the most, including their biological fathers, stepfathers and maternal uncles. Victims of defilement and incest were found to be as young as three years, the average age being 13 years. The perpetrators were much older than the victims and ranged in age from 16 years to 72 years. The majority of them were in their early twenties and thirties. It was not uncommon, however, for minors to rape their fellow minors.

The incidences of incest (and defilement) took place at any time of the day, although younger victims were more likely to be abused during the day and older ones at night. The findings also showed that in most cases the perpetrator enticed, assaulted and threatened the victim into submission. In the cases of younger victims, they would be enticed with sweets and small amounts of money.

The study revealed that there are no standardised police procedures in handling cases of violence against women. Procedures varied from police station to police station, a practice that is very confusing to the public. It should be noted that the violence against women sector of the Women's NGO Coalition, of which WLSA is a member, drafted a proposed legislation on family violence which was presented in Parliament in 1999 as a Private Member's Bill. The proposed legislation included procedures for handling cases of violence against women. WLSA took the initiative by taking the proposed legislation to the public and other stakeholders such as the police, magistrates, doctors, tribal leaders, social workers and other NGOs, to seek their input. The result of this exercise was a revised version of the proposed police procedures, which has since been submitted to the Commissioner of Police for consideration (see Appendix 2)

Police records showed that the complainants withdrew many cases before they reached the courts. The most common reason for withdrawals was that the family of the perpetrator and that of the victim knew each other, and they would settle the matter at family level. This occurred despite all the time, effort and other resources the police put into the investigations and the strong feeling that they could secure a conviction. However, a directive from the Police Commissioner now requires the police not to allow complainants to withdraw cases at the police station but rather to take the matter to the magistrate court. The magistrate would then use her or his discretion to terminate or continue the case.

It was evident from police records that medical evidence provided by doctors for the most part did not serve the purpose it was meant to. Where doctors were required to give a report of the medical condition of the victim, they instead provided a legal opinion which is the prerogative of the magistrates. Notwithstanding this, the police form B.P.73, which provides medical evidence in cases of violence, was found inadequate and outdated. During the course of this study, WLSA, with the participation of the various stakeholders, including the police, medical doctors, nurses, magistrates, social workers, teachers, state attorneys and NGOs, reviewed the form. The form was made gender sensitive by removing presently degrading requirements to prove that women have been raped such as the insertion of fingers into the woman's vagina and all questions irrelevant to the violence, such as the victim's sex life, were removed. The revised version was submitted to the Commissioner of Police. Both the original and the revised medical forms B.P.73 are presented in Appendix 3.

Whereas the police have been mandated to prosecute in all sexual offence cases without deferring to the Attorney General's Chambers, in cases of incest they have to obtain approval to prosecute from the Attorney General. This delays the hearing of such cases and has a negative impact on victims. Victims, particularly those of incest, in the mean time continue to reside in the same abusive home due to lack of places of safety as provided for by the Children's Act. In addition, the needs of the victims are not taken into account. No counselling services are provided within the government structures. Where NGOs provide counselling, it is inadequate due to lack of specialised counselling skills.

9.2. Recommendations

Based on the findings of the study – discussions with study informants as well as literature consulted – it is clear that the issue of child sexual abuse is complex and therefore requires an interdisciplinary approach to solve the problem. Intervention requires political will, combined and coordinated efforts of state and non-state institutions, people of different professional backgrounds, and the community at large. This chapter presents some suggestions for addressing the problem of child sexual abuse. Emphasis is placed on legal reforms as well as reforms affecting matters of procedure when handling cases of incest and defilement, and citizen empowerment in general.

9.2.1 Law Reform
Several provisions by the existing laws that are pertinent to the subject of sexual abuse of women and the girl-child need to be rethought and amended accordingly. Key among these are provisions that deal with the definition of a child, definition of sexual abuse, including its rape, incest and defilement compo-

nents, the prosecution of cases, and the punishment of offenders.

Definition of Child
As evident from this study, the law is often conflicting when it comes to the definition of who is a child (see Chapter 2). To remove the inconsistencies in the various statutes and to harmonise the law and make it to more effectively serve the purpose for which it was legislated this study recommends that:

> *The definition of the child presented in the Convention on the Rights of the Child, of which Botswana is a signatory, be adopted for all purposes. This means that the cut-off age for who is a child should be 18 years of age.*

Sexual Abuse: Rape, Incest and Defilement
Some of the acts of sexual abuse in the Penal Code are rape, defilement and incest. Rape is defined in terms of penetration of 'a sexual organ or any instrument, of whatever nature, into the person of another for the purposes of sexual gratification...' (Penal Code (Amendment) Act, 1998, 141:08:01). By extension, penetration forms part of the definitions of incest and defilement. There are other forms of sexual abuse that do not necessarily involve penetration such as touching or forcing a person to touch his or her genitals, the genitals of others or of the perpetrator. Such acts can be as traumatic to the victim as rape. To make the law more inclusive and effective as a tool for the protection of general sexual abuse the following recommendations are put forth:

> *The law should be amended to include sexually abusive practices, such as touching or forcing a person to touch one's genitals, the genitals of others or of the perpetrator, which are not catered for in its existing form. It should not be left to the discretion of the police to classify such acts as attempted rape or indecent assault as is presently the case. Indeed, these sexual offences should fall under the same category as rape.*

With particular reference to incest, the study showed that the current law is problematic with respect to the definition of this crime and the penalty prescribed for offenders. Not only does the Penal Code provide for what amounts to a narrow list of relatives who can perpetuate incest, it also stipulates what passes for a lenient sentence for the perpetrators of the crime. Consistent with the sentiments expressed by respondents of our study, it is strongly recommended that:

The Penal Code should be amended to broaden the list of relatives who can be liable to a charge of incest to include maternal and paternal uncles, maternal and paternal aunts, and cousins.

The penalty for incest should be revised. The current law provides a maximum of 5 years imprisonment with no provision for HIV testing. In the case of defilement the penalty is between ten years and life imprisonment and HIV testing is mandatory where one is found guilty. It is recommended that the penalty for incest be the same as that for defilement.

As applies to defilement, the law is particularly problematic with respect to the cut-off age at which the offence could be judged to have been committed. The use of the term 'unlawful' in the definition of defilement in the law is rather misleading. To correct these anomalies and others earlier discussed, we suggest the following:

That, in view of the recommendation put forth earlier, that the cut-off age for the dfinition of a child should be 18 years, the law on defilement be amended to state that it is a crime for any person to have sexual intercourse with any other person under the age of 18 years.

That the term 'unlawful', as is the case at current definition, should be removed as it suggests that there are times when it is 'lawful' to sexually abuse children.

That under no circumstances should any person under the age of 18 years be allowed to marry. We, however, acknowledge the fact that the Government is in the process of amending the Marriage Act.

That the practice by the police to classify sexual abuse of under age persons as rape should be brought to an end because it conceals the fact that adults in our society sexually abuse children. This, in turn, makes society fail to acknowledge its responsibility and thus fail to address the problem.

Medical Provisions
For laws addressing offences of sexual abuse to be more effective and well-rounded, they should be designed and implemented as tools for not only preventing sexual crimes themselves, but also for governing possible negative repercussions of offences on the victims such as unwanted pregnancies and in-

fection with HIV/AIDS. To facilitate this it is recommended that:

> *The current laws should be amended to incorporate medical provisions governing the prevention of possible unwanted pregnancies and addressing the possibility of contracting HIV/AIDS. More specifically, it is suggested that the law should be improved to:*
>
>> *Provide for the morning after pill free of charge to victims who are at risk of getting pregnant, with the objective of preventing possible unwanted pregnancies. Moreover, such a law should also provide that doctors inform victims of the availability of the morning after pill.*
>>
>> *Require the Government to provide HIV 'cocktail' drugs free of chage to all victims of sexual abuse in order to reduce the risk of being infected with HIV.*

Legislation on Family/Domestic Violence
One of the impediments to the prevention of family/domestic violence is the lack of a broad law that is specific to the subject matter. The Penal Code does not address itself to issues in this area. Although the Penal Code was amended in 1998 in an attempt to make it gender neutral, the laws that are gender neutral assume that all persons are equal in all ways: legally, socially, economically and culturally. As discussed in the findings chapters of this study, however, the position of women and girl-children according to general and customary laws and practices in Botswana, is subordinate to that of men. This position makes them vulnerable to the power and authority of men, exposing them to violence by men, including sexual abuse.

It is in light of the above situation that the members of the Women's NGO Coalition prepared proposed legislation on family violence which was presented in Parliament in 1999 as a Private Member's Bill. As a follow up to this endeavour, this study strongly recommends that:

> *The Bill on family violence should be passed into law without further delay. Once it becomes law, its provisions should be implemented and monitored to the letter in order to guarantee that women's vulnerability to domestic violence in our society is reduced significantly.*

9.2.2 Legal Service Interventions
Legal service interventions should focus on matters of procedure when han-

dling cases of sexual abuse. In particular, they should focus on strengthening the family, the police, social welfare and medical personnel, NGOs and the business community as agents for the prevention of sexual offences.

The Family
In view of the study findings that, contrary to expectations, the family is not necessarily a safe haven for children, it is recommended that:

> *Under no circumstances should cases of incest and defilement be referred back from the police to the family for conflict resolutions. These crimes should be removed from the private sphere into the public sphere.*
>
> *Where the child victim was sexually abused by a parent or any other person with whom she shares the same homestead, and while awaiting trial, she should be removed to a safer place. Social workers should thoroughly explore other alternatives instead of the child being returned to the same abusive home.*

The Police
To reduce incidences of sexual abuse in our society it is imperative that the police improve their performance and double their initiatives in combating the types of offences associated with it. This applies to police involvement in both the investigation and prosecution of sex offences, the procedures available for handling cases, and the reliance on medical form B.P.73 as a major prosecution weapon.

(i) *Investigative Skills.* To enhance police investigative skills, this study recommends that:

> *The police should be adequately trained in investigative skills and evidence gathering so as to reduce their reliance on witnesses. There are cases where police fail to prosecute due to uncooperative victims and witnesses who refuse to provide evidence. As in murder cases, appropriate tools such as cameras should be utilised by the police at the scene of sexual crimes and for injuries sustained as part of evidence gathering.*

(ii) *Prosecution of Cases.* To enhance and speed up the prosecution of cases of incest and defilement, we recommend that:

The practice of referring incest cases to the Attorney General's Chambers for approval of prosecution by the police should be done away with because it delays the hearing of such cases and has a negative impact on victims. Such cases should be dealt with in the same manner as other sexual abuse cases.

(iii) *Police Procedures for Handling Cases of Sexual Violence.* A great source of concern in the handling of incest and defilement cases in Botswana is the lack of standardised police procedures. In addition, the current approach used in handling cases of violence is fragmented with various related services provided by different government departments which have different agendas for addressing the same problem. For instance, doctors are more concerned with treatment of the victim than collecting medical evidence to assist the police. Because of this, the police are disadvantaged in their gathering of evidence. The lack of standardised police procedures is also partially to blame for the low rate in the reporting of rape, incest and defilement offences.

To circumvent the above dilemmas, we recommend the following:

That standardised police procedures should be put in place as a matter of urgency. In this respect, the proposed police procedures submitted to the Commissioner of Police by the WLSA Research Trust should be adopted and implemented. Such procedures should form part of the training of the police as they join the service.

That the police should adopt an integrated approach whereby, at least at district level, they have medical doctors, nurses, psychologists, social workers, counsellors, forensic laboratories and technicians, and lawyers within their structure.

That police procedures in handling cases of violence should be written in simplified English and Setswana and made available to the public. They should also be made easily accessible by placing them at reception areas of police community services centres and public places such as shops, schools, clinics, hospitals and at the offices of other government departments. In addition, these should be made victim friendly to avoid the tendency for them to traumatise victims further.

(iv) *Medical Form B.P.73*. Central to the successful prosecution of rape, incest and defilement cases is the medical report provided by doctors on form B.P.73. As it is currently structured, however, the form has been an ineffective prosecution tool. To say the least, form B.P.73 is outdated, particularly in view of the Penal Code (Amendment) Act 1998. It is inadequate and unclear as to what criteria is used to suggest that a victim had been raped. To improve the quality of reports realised through the completion of form B.P.73, this study suggests that:

> *The revised version of the police form B.P.73 which WLSA submitted to the Commissioner of Police should be adopted and implemented without further delay.*

> *The police hold workshops with doctors countrywide to sensitise doctors on the role they play in providing the police with medical evidence in cases of violence. As evident from the findings of the study, doctors do not currently seem to appreciate the importance of their role in the successful prosecution of, and consequently, the prevention of, incest and defilement offences.*

Medical Personnel
As alluded to above, medical reports form part of police evidence and are thus crucial in the conviction or otherwise of perpetrators. To strengthen such reports, our study recommends that doctors should:

> *Attend to victims of defilement and incest promptly to avoid the loss of very important medical pointers that the crime of rape, incest or defilement actually took place.*

> *Write their reports in a legible manner for the benefit of the police and magistrates. This is necessary if police are to utilise such reports effectively to strengthen their cases against accused persons.*

> *Avoid giving legal opinion because their responsibility is to provide facts about the medical condition of the victim at the time of examination. Giving legal opinion in these matters is the mandate of judicial officers.*

Non-Governmental Organizations
Non-governmental organizations are in the forefront of providing the much needed legal aid services in cases of violence, particularly against women and

children. These are very few and concentrated in Gaborone, and consequently not easily accessible to the majority of people. Moreover, they face problems of human, financial and other resources to enable them to reach out to more people. Nevertheless, such NGOs can play a more effective role in combating sexual violence. By way of facilitating this, our study recommends that:

In view of the fact that the proposed Protection from Domestic Violence Act has already been drafted and presented to Parliament as a Private Member's Bill – the member sponsoring the bill has since been appointed to the cabinet – members of the Women's NGO Coalition should lobby vigorously for its enactment.

NGOs should spread their bases. Currently, most NGOs are based and concentrate their services in and around Gaborone. As such, many people have to travel long distances with limited resources to access services provided by these NGOs. Thus, depending on the services provided, NGOs should set up other bases beyond Gaborone so that their services are accessible to the wider community. Without any strings attached except for NGOs to utilise funds for the purposes for which they were sought, Government should financially assist NGOs in this endeavour.

NGOs should network and closely collaborate in their endeavours to tackle the menace of domestic violence. There are a number of NGOs mandated to address various aspects of violence in Botswana. Although much has been achieved, a lot still remains to be done. In the past, and through the violence against women sector of the Women's NGO Coalition, this was done through close collaboration and co-ordination of efforts. This networking needs to be revitalised if further progress on the situation of women and girl-children is to be realised.

All NGOs, particularly women's ones, should facilitate gender training for their members. Currently, different NGOs have different agendas. What they have in common, however, is the will to promote the rights of women and girl-children as human rights. Notwithstanding, some members or employees of these organizations are not gender sensitive, and tend to provide information or advice that perpetuates patriarchal values.

The Business Community
The business community must have a significant role to play in the eradication

of violence against women and children as part of their service to the community. To bring them on board, this study recommends that:

The business community provide financial and other support to NGOs in combating violence against women and girl-children since their (women's and children's) suffering negatively affects productivity and, consequently, national development.

9.2.3 Intervention Programmes for Victims

In the process of dealing with offences of incest and defilement, the needs of the victims particularly those dealing with safety and counselling, are not adequately taken into account.

Places of Safety
It is often the case that victims of sexual abuse have nowhere safe to stay. Hence the title of this study, 'No Safe Place...'. To guarantee the victims of sexual violence places of safety it is recommended that:

The Government should provide places of safety throughout the country for abused children. Such places should not be the sole responsibility of NGOs like SOS or the Women's Shelter which have limited resources and run on tight budgets.

Counselling
The majority of children who are victims of incest and defilement attend school and spend a lot of their time at school. Therefore, it is suggested that:

The guidance and counselling programmes within schools should be treated as an essential part of the mainstream curriculum instead of being treated as an extra-curricula activity.

All guidance and counselling teachers should be equipped with appropriate skills to enable them to provide counselling to those students needing assistance as well as identifying problems where they exist.

The Postgraduate Diploma on Counsellor Education offered by the Department of Educational Foundations at the University of Botswana should be part of the basic courses offered by the Department of Social Work at undergraduate level. This will enhance the preparation of social workers as han-

dlers of victims of rape, incest and defilement.

Counsellors should be employed at police stations, clinics and hospitals to provide immediate services to victims.

9.2.4 Citizen Empowerment

The findings of the study showed that, more often than not, perpetrators of incest and defilement are members of the same community against whom they direct their violent acts. In order to address this problem, it is necessary to provide legal education to the members of the community, sensitise them and raise their awareness about the value of reporting such crimes to law enforcement authorities.

Legal Education
Legal awareness and knowledge is pertinent to reducing the incest and defilement offences that are rampant in our society. Thus:

The Government should take the lead in disseminating information on laws and procedures pertaining to violence against women, incest and defilement;

Laws should be translated into simple language for the benefit of all. Most laws are written in a legal language which is not easily understandable by people without a legal background. It should be the responsibility of the Government to ensure the simplification of laws. This could be attained by using less technical English and by translating the same into Setswana. Government can also financially support initiatives by NGOs interested in undertaking the exercise. Such simplified laws should be distributed countrywide.

All NGOs working in the area of law should provide legal education to their counterparts who are focusing on non-legal areas. Also, where relevant, legal expertise is not available within particular NGOs, they should seek the services of others. These steps are important because, whatever their focus or agenda, issues of violence affect all NGOs and the populations they serve.

Sensitization and Awareness Raising
A key revelation by this study was that, in Botswana, as elsewhere in the world,

the crimes of incest and defilement remain grossly under-reported. Part of this under-reporting can be explained in terms of the lack of awareness among victims and other community members. To address this problem, this study recommends that:

> *In line with the concept of community policing, the members of different communities should be sensitised to the fact that they can report cases of sexual abuse of children without fear of legal action being taken against them. The law should provide for this explicitly. The police, in conjunction with any citizen, or state- or non-state institutions, including NGOs, should spearhead the awareness raising campaigns.*

By way of concluding, it should be reiterated that the recommendations presented above are necessary if the war against violence against women and girl-children in general, and sexual abuse in particular, is going to move closer to being won. Their implementation, however, requires political will on the part of our policy makers. In particular, Parliament should demonstrate its commitment to the safety and wellbeing of its people, especially its children. Members should be proactive in legal reform. Where motions for law reform regarding the situation of women and girl-children are made, members should rise above their cultural and other biases, of whatever nature, and focus on their role in enhancing the human condition. Cabinet ministers should ensure that their ministries implement programmes in a timely and satisfactory manner. If the political leaders display a sense of justice, commitment and responsibility towards all, irrespective of gender, then implementation of all recommendations will be achievable.

Appendix 1: Tables

TABLE A1: POLICE STATIONS, CUSTOMARY COURTS AND MAGISTRATE COURTS VISITED

Sites	Greater Gaborone	Greater Francistown
Police Stations	Gaborone West	Tatitown
	Broadhurst	Kutlwano
	Old Naledi	Tonota
	Mogoditshane	Tutume
	Mochudi	Masunga
Customary Courts	Gaborone West	Tatitown
	Old Naledi	Kutlwano
	Mogoditshane	Tonota
	Mochudi	Tutume
		Masunga
Magistrate Courts	Gaborone West	Francistown
	Broadhurst	Masunga
	Mochudi	

TABLE A2: NUMBER OF FOCUS GROUP PARTICIPANTS BY CATEGORY AND GENDER

Category	Male	Female	Total
Students	122	138	260
Police	42	9	51
Tribal Leaders	49	4	53
Total	**213**	**151**	**364**

TABLE A3: NUMBER OF STUDENT RESPONDENTS BY SCHOOL AND GENDER

Study Area	School	Males	Females	Total
Greater Gaborone	Ledumang SSS	6	6	12
	Marang CJSS	10	6	16
	Gaborone SSS	19	14	33
	Sir Seretse CJSS	5	7	12
	Mogoditshane CJSS	18	21	39
	St Joseph's College (SSS)	7	13	20
	Molefi SSS	3	7	10
Greater Francistown	Mater Spei College (SSS)	4	9	13
	Shashe River SSS	7	12	19
	Tonota CJSS	9	10	19
	Tutume McConnel SSS	10	10	20
	Denjebuya CJSS	9	7	16
	Masunga SSS	5	6	11
	Maruje CJSS	10	10	20
Total		**122**	**138**	**260**

CJSS – Community Junior Secondary School; SSS – Senior Secondary School

TABLE A4: NUMBER OF POLICE OFFICERS PARTICIPATING IN GROUP DISCUSSIONS BY STATION AND GENDER

Police Station	Male	Female	Total
Old Naledi	5	4	9
Broadhurst	3	1	4
Gaborone West	4	0	4
Gaborone Central	5	0	5
Mochudi	10	4	14
Tatitown	11	0	11
Tonota	4	0	4
Total	**42**	**9**	**51**

TABLE A5: NUMBER OF TRIBAL LEADERS PARTICIPATING IN GROUP DISCUSSION BY AREA AND GENDER

Area	Male	Female	Total
Mogoditshane	9	0	9
Mochudi	3	0	3
Tutume	4	0	4
Francistown	1	2	3
Tonota	9	0	9
Masunga	23	2	25
Total	**49**	**4**	**53**

TABLE A6: NUMBER OF WORKSHOP PARTICIPANTS BY RESEARCH AREA

Category of Respondents	Greater Gaborone	Greater Francistown	Total
Police	10	24	34
Health workers	3	5	8
Social workers	4	8	12
State Attorneys	0	1	1
Magistrates	0	3	3
Teachers	0	2	2
Media	0	3	3
NGOs	13	5	18
Total	**30**	**51**	**81**

TABLE A7: KEY INFORMANTS BY AREA OF STUDY

Greater Gaborone	Greater Francistown
Director – Metlhaetsile	Social Worker – Masunga
Coordinator – Kagisano Women's Shelter	Social Worker – Nyangabgwe Hospital
House Mother and Counsellor – Kagisano	Coordinator – SOS Francistown
Coordinator – Child Line	Principal Medical Officer – Masunga Hospital
Deputy Attorney General	
Social Worker – Tirelo Sechaba	Obstetrician/Gynaecologist – Nyangabgwe Hospital
	Station Commander – Masunga Police
	Head-Nurse – Botswelelo Clinic, Francistown
	Head Nurse – Tonota Clinic

Appendix 2: Proposed Police Procedures on Family/Domestic Violence

1. Occurrence Book
When a **Police Officer** receives a request/complaint that domestic/family violence has or is likely to occur, he/she will record the complaint in an **occurrence book.**

2. Written Statement
It is **mandatory** for the Police Officer to record complainants of domestic/family violence. The complainant shall be given a copy of his/her statement in any one of the official languages according to the preference of the victim.

3. Medical Attention
The **Police Officer** shall ensure that the victim of violence receives immediate medical attention at the nearest appropriate medical facility.

4. Appropriate Medical Report
It is the responsibility of the **Police Officer** to ensure that the doctor makes a report relevant to the victim's complaint.

5. Photographs of Injuries
Where the victim has sustained physical injuries, the police shall ensure that photographs are immediately taken.

6. Mandatory Arrest of the Accused
The **accused** shall be arrested until the victim receives a **protection order.**

7. Investigations
Upon receiving the complaint, the police shall, as soon as possible, investigate the allegations against the accused.

8. Essential Assistance to the Victim
The **Police Officer** is obliged to inform the victim of his/her right to seek assistance in the following manner:

A. *Court Order*
   (i) A court order may be obtained from the magistrate court free of charge. The order seeks to prevent further abuse of the victim and her children by the abuser.

The order can be a protection order, tenancy or occupation order.

   (ii) The victim may request the magistrate not to disclose his/her new address to the abuser.
   (iii) The order may direct the abuser to pay the victim emergency financial assistance, and desist from any contact with the victim and the children.
   (iv) The order may evict the abuser from the home or direct the abuser to allow the victim and the children access to the home.

Important! The **Police Officer** shall explain that the order is only temporary, and the victim would have to go to court at a later date to make the order more permanent.

B. *Temporary shelter and transportation*
   (i) The **Police Officer** may assist the victim in identifying temporary residence/shelter for herself/himself and the children, which may include the home of a family member or friend. The **Police Officer** shall also provide the victim with transport to the alternative residence if required to do so.
   (ii) The **Police Officer** shall accompany the victim to his/her previous residence to collect personal belongings if the need arises.

C. *Counselling and Support Sources*
   The **Police Officer** shall give the victim information on different groups for victims of domestic violence, and organizations that provide counselling services and similar services within the victim's locality.

D. *Criminal Complaint*
   (i) Where the accused commits any other criminal offence against the victim or children, the **Police Officer** must inform the victim of his/her right to make a criminal complaint against the accused.
   (ii) The **Police Officer** must inform the victim of his/her right to institute additional criminal proceedings against the accused, where the accused has breached the *protection, tenancy or occupation order.*

The complaint must be made as soon as possible, as otherwise the victim may be prevented from making the complaint at a future date.

E. Prosecution for False Statements
The **Police Officer** shall warn the victim that any false statement made in the *protection order* or criminal complaint will amount to an offence which can lead to the victim's prosecution.

9. Copy of Victim's Rights
The **Police Officer** shall give the victim a copy of his/her rights as stated in (8) above in any one of the official languages according to the preference of the victim.

10. No Option of Fine
When charged with an offence of domestic/family violence, the accused shall not be given an option to make an admission of guilt fine in lieu of arrest.

11. Costs
No order of costs shall be granted against any party to the proceedings.

12. Conviction
Upon conviction, the accused is liable either to a fine or imprisonment or both.

Appendix 3: The Original and Proposed Revised Medical Form B.P.73

Currently Used Forms

Report on Examination in a Case of Alleged Assault or Other Crime   B.P. 73

THIS FORM IS TO BE USED BY MEDICAL OFFICERS AND MEDICAL PRACTITIONERS MAKING AN EXAMINATION FOR THE GOVERNMENT

Form "A" should be completed in all cases including rape and post-mortem examinations where injuries are found and form "B" should be submitted in cases where a female has been examined in connection with a sexual offence.

This is to Certify that at the request of ([1])...

I have this ([2])............day of...................19..... at the hour of...............m

examined at([3])..the person of

([4]).. and have to report as follows:—

Sex.............. Apparent Age........... Race ....

State of the person as regards physical powers and general state of health.....................

....

....

Condition of Clothing..

....

Bruises and Abrasions (if any) ([5])..

....

Wounds (if any) ([6])...

....

....

Any other Injuries ([6]) ....

State of Organs of Generation (of examined) ([6])..

....

Miscroscopical or other Special Examination of States, etc. ([7]).........................

....

....

....

Remarks..

....

....

Place........................   ....
                                   Medical Officer, or Medical Practitioner

---

([1]) Name of official or person at whose instance the examination was carried out.
([2]) Date and hour of conducting the examination.
([3]) Place where examination was carried out.
([4]) Name of person examined.
([5]) In every case the nature, position and extent of the abrasion, wound, or other injury must be exactly described, together with its probable date and manner of causation, any apparent discrepancy between any statement made by the person and the conditions actually found on examination being noted.
([6]) In the case of a female her consent, or, if a minor, the consent of her lawful guardian, should be first obtained especially if the examination is undertaken in connection with a charge of infanticide or concealment of birth.
([7]) If any vomit or excreta or portion of clothing or other article is taken for special examination, its nature should be noted here and the manner of its preservation and disposal stated.

No Safe Place

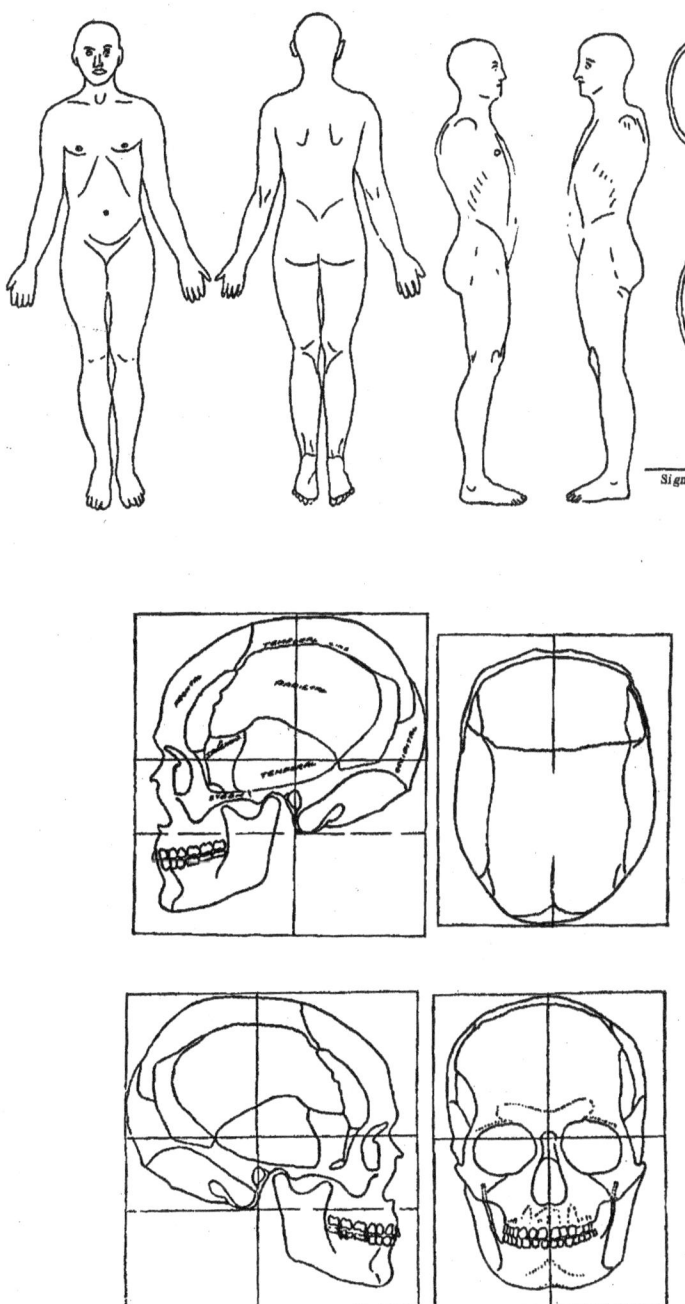

Signature

REPORT ON EXAMINATION IN A CASE OF ALLEGED RAPE OR OTHER SEXUAL OFFENCE

Name... Race..................... Age......

Physical Condition........................... Mental State.............................

Sex Life ....

Menstruation.................................. Pregnancies..........................

....

Assault...

....

Injuries: (Extragenital)..

....

Breasts..	**OPINION**
Labia Majora	
Labia Minora	
Vestibule	
Hymen...	
Vagina: (1,2,3 Fingers)........................	
Fourchette	
Perineum	
Discharge.....................................	
Haemorrhage..................................	
Examination (Easy—painful)....................	
Uterus..	
Vaginal Smears	

Remarks:—

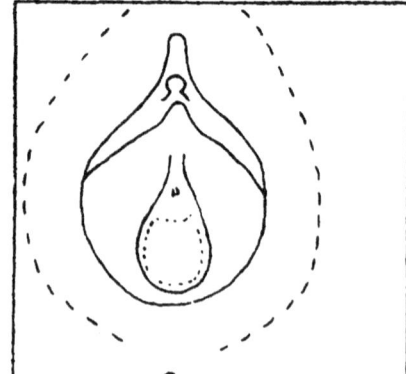

Signature................................

Proposed Forms

NO SAFE PLACE

FORM A

Report on Examination in a Case of Alleged Assault or Other Crime

THIS FORM IS TO BE USED BY MEDICAL OFFICERS AND MEDICAL PRACTITIONERS MAKING AN EXAMINATION FOR THE GOVERNMENT

Form 'A' should be completed in all cases, including rape and post-mortem examinations where injuries are found, and forms B, C and BP 73 Insert should be completed in cases where a person has been examined in connection with a sexual offence. BP 73 Insert should be submitted to the lab with exhibits collected from the examination.

This is to certify that at the request of (^{1}) ....

I have this () .... day of .... 20 .... at the hour of ....

examined at () ....(^{2}) ....

....Sex.......................Age...............................

State of the person as regards physical and general state of health..

....

Condition of clothing ....

....

Bruises and Abrasions (if any) ....

....

....

Wounds (if any) (^{3}) ....

....

....

Any other injuries..

State organs of generation (of examined) ....

....

....

Special Investigation (^{4}) ....

....

....

Remarks ....

....

....

....

Place... ....

Medical Officer or Medical Practitioner

---

[1] Name of official at whose instance the examination was carried out. It should be understood that such request is made on behalf of the Station Commander
[2] Date and hour of conducting the examination.
[3] Place where examination was carried out.
[4] Name of person examined.
[5] In every case the nature, position and extent of the abrasions, wounds, or other injuries must be exactly described, together with their probable date and manner of causation, any apparent descrepancy between any statement made by the person and the conditions actually found on examination being noted.
[6] Consent must be obtained from the person being examined or, in the case of a minor from his/her legal guardian.
[7] Special investigations done: vomit, excreta, X-rays, etc.

No Safe Place

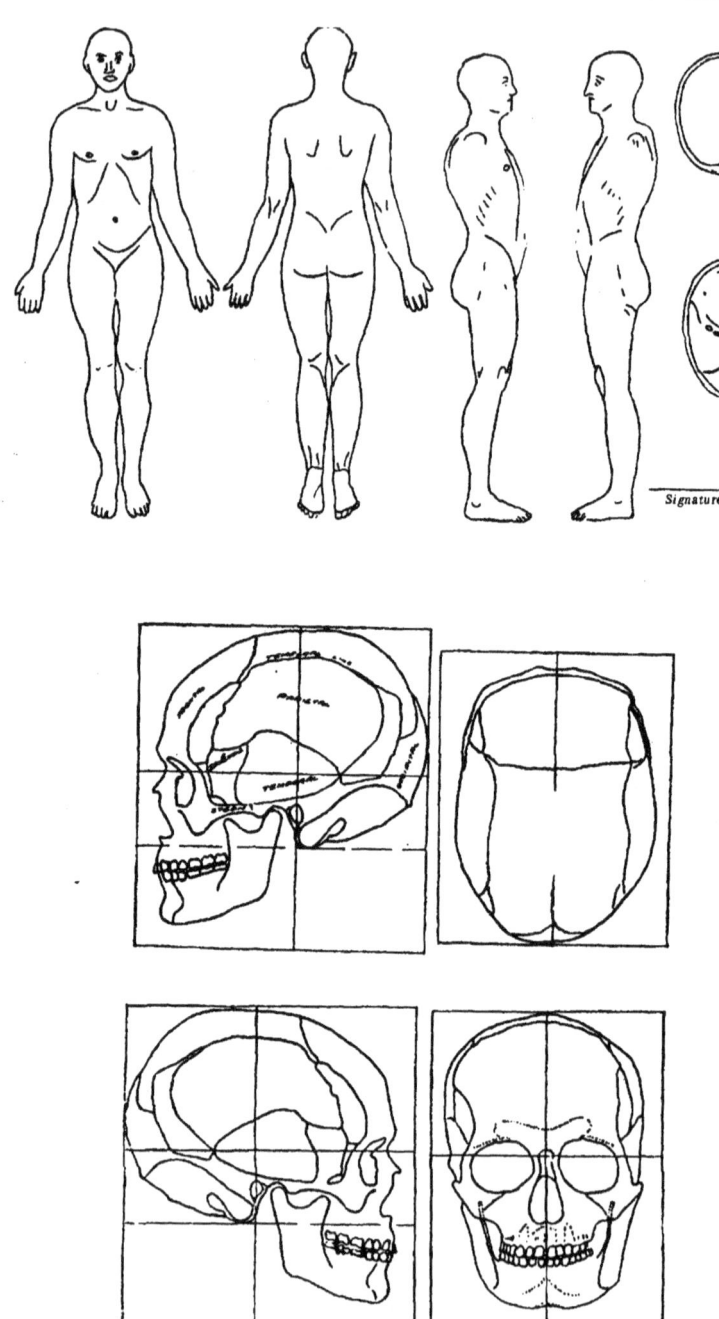

No Safe Place

FORM B

Report on Examination in a Case of Alleged Rape or Other Sexual Offence for either Female or Male (where applicable)

Have you had sexual intercourse before? ....

When was your last menstruation? .... Are you pregnant? ....

....

Breast injuries ....

....

Genital injuries (Specify) ....

....

....

....

Hymen ....   **OPINION**

Penis/Vagina ....   **(After Conclusive Investigation)**

....

Vaginal smears...   ....

Anus ....

....

Uterus ....

....

Rectal examination ....

....

Discharge ....

Internal examination (Easy – Painful) ....

Blood group ....

HIV test done ....

Other STDs e.g. ,VDRL ....

BRIEF SUMMARY

....

....

....

....

....

....

....

Signature ....   Date ....

BIBLIOGRAPHY

Bagley, C. and Thomlinson, (eds.). 1991.*Child Sexual Abuse: Critical Perspectives on Prevention, Intervention and Treatment.* Toronto: Wall and Emerson.
Becker, J. V. 1994. 'Offenders: Characteristics and Treatment.' *The Future of Children,* 4: 176 – 197.
Black, H. C. (ed.). 1979. *Black's Law Dictionary.* St. Paul, MN: West Publishers.
Botswana Family Welfare Association (BOFWA). 1997. *Child Abuse.* Gaborone: Botswana Printing and Publishing.
Botswana Gazette, Wednesday, 15 July 1998: p.3.
Botswana Guardian, Friday, 24, January, 1997: p.1.
Botswana Guardian, Friday, 9 August 1996: p.1.
Botswana Police Service. 1997. *A Report Submitted by the Police Task Force in Response to Cases of Domestic Violence.* Gaborone: Botswana Police.
Botswana Police Service. 1999. *A Report of a Study on Rape in Botswana.* Gaborone: Botswana Police.
Boyle, J. 1992. *Critical Legal Studies.* Aldershot: Dartmouth.
Central Statistics Office. 1997. *The 1996 Botswana Family Health Survey III.* Gaborone: Department of Printing and Publishing Services.
Central Statistics Office. 1999. *Education Statistics 1998.* Gaborone, Department of Printing and Publishing Services.
Check, W.A. 1989. *The Encyclopedia of Health, Child Abuse.* USA: Chelsea House Publishers.
Cleveland, D. 1986. *Incest. The Story of Three Women.* Massachusetts: Heath and Company.
Deltufo, A. 1995. *Domestic Violence for Beginners.* London: Writers and Readers Publishing.
Dobash, R. and Dobash R. 1979. *Violence Against Wives.* New York: Free Press.
Dow, U. 2000. 'Legal Aspects – HIV/AIDS: Care, Counselling and Research.' A Paper Presented at the December 2000, Botswana–Harvard Partnership for Research and Education Workshop. (Unpublished).
Driver, E. 1989. *Child Sexual Abuse: A Feminist Reader.* New York: New York University Press.
Goode, J. 1993. *World Changes in Divorce Patterns.* London: Yale University Press.
Government of Botswana. *The Children's Act, Chapter 28.04.* Gaborone: Government Printers.
Griffiths, J. 1986. 'What is Legal Pluralism?' *Journal of Legal Pluralism,* 24:1
Hanmer, J., Radford, J. and Stanko E. A. (Eds.). 1989. *Women, Policing and Male Violence: Internal Perspective.* London: Routledge.
Hunt K, and Kitzinger J. 1996. 'Public Place, Private Issue? The Public's Reaction to the Zero Tolerance Campaign against Violence against Women'. In Bradby, H. (ed.) *Defining Violence: Understanding the Causes and Effects of Violence.* Vermont: Avebury.
Johnson, A. G. 1995. *The Blackwell Dictionary of Sociology. A User's Guide to Sociological Language.* Cambridge: Basil Blackwell Inc.
Justice, B. and Justice, R. 1979. *The Broken Taboo. Sex in the Family.* London: Peter Owen.

Loewenson, R. 1997. *Sexual Abuse of Children in Zimbabwe*. Harare, Zimbabwe.
Mackinnon, C. A. 1987. *Feminism Unmodified*. Cambridge: Harvard University Press.
Mmegi/The Reporter, Vol. 13, no 11, 22–28 March 1996: p8.
Midweek Sun, Wednesday, 8 April 1998: p. 7
Midweek Sun, Wednesday 22 July 1998: p. 3
Molokomme, A. 1991. 'Children of the Fence: The Maintenance of Extra-marital Children Under Law and Practice in Botswana. Research Report No 41'. University of Leiden African Studies Centre, The Netherlands.
Molokomme, A. 1994. 'Customary Law in Botswana: Past, Present and Future'. In Brothers, H. and Brothers, N., *Botswana in the 21st Century*, Gaborone: Botswana Society.
Molokomme, A. and Mokobi, K. 1998. 'Custody and Guardianship of Children in Botswana. Customary Laws and Judicial Practice within the Framework of the Children's Convention'. In Ncube, W. (ed.), *Law, Culture, Tradition and Children's Rights in Eastern and Southern Africa*. Brookfield, USA: Ashgate.
Moore, S. F. 1973. 'Law and Social Change: The Semi-Autonomous Social Fields as an Appropriate Field of Study'. *Law and Society Review* 7:719.
Murdock, G. P. 1949. *Social Structures*. New York: Macmillan,
National Institute for Public Interest Law and Research (NIPILAR).1996. *We Won't be Beaten. A Guide to the Prevention of Family Violence Act*. Community Centre (South Africa).
Ncube, W. 1998. 'Prospects and Challenges in Eastern and Southern Africa'. In *Law, Culture and Tradition in Eastern and Southern Africa*. Brookfield, USA: Ashgate.
Newman, D. M. 1995. *Sociology. Exploring the Architecture of Everyday Life*. Thousand Oaks, CA.: Pine Forge Press.
Perez de Cuellar, J. UN Secretary-General, in a message to the International Meeting on the Convention on the Rights of the Child, Lignano, Italy, September 1987. From UNICEF. 'Girls and Boys on Equal Terms'. Background Note No.6. *Convention on the Rights of the Child. Briefing Kit*. New York: Centre for Human Rights: United Nations.
Renvoize, J. 1982. *Incest. A Family Pattern*. London: Routledge and Kegan Paul.
Roberts, S. and Comaroff, J. 1971. 'Marriage and Extra-Marital Sexuality: The Dialectics of Legal Change among the Kgatla'. *Journal of African Law*. Vol. 21: 1.
Schaefer, R.T. and Lamm, R.P. 1995. *Sociology*. (5th ed.). New York: McGraw-Hill.
Spies, K.B. 1992. *Everything You Need to Know About Incest*. New York: Rosen Publishing Group.
Spike, P.V and Sission Runyan, A. 1993. 'The Gender of World Politics'. In *Global Gender Issues*. Boulder, Colorado: Westview Press.
Tabengwa, M. and Fergus, I.M. 1998. 'Violence Against Women'. A Paper Presented at The First National Crime Prevention Conference, 2nd – 4th February 1998.
UNICEF. n.d.*Convention on the Rights of the Child. Briefing Kit*. New York: Centre for Human Rights: United Nations.
United Nations. 1993. *Strategies for Confronting Domestic Violence. A Resource Manual*. New York: United Nations.
United Nations. 1996. *Platform for Action and the Beijing Declaration*. New York: United Nations.
United Nations. 1989. *Convention on the Rights of the Child*. New York: United Nations.
Van der Mey, B. J. and Neff, R. L. 1986. *Incest as Child Abuse. Research and Applications*. New

York: Praeger.
Visvanathan, N. 1997 'Introduction'. In Visvanathan, N., Duggan, L, Nisonoff. L and Wiegersma, N (eds.), *The Women, Gender and Development Reader.* Dhaka: Dhaka University Press
Watts, C. et. al. 1997. "Women, Violence and HIV/AIDS in Zimbabwe" S*AfAIDS News,* Vol.5 No.2: 2–6.
Wilson, K.J. 1997. *When Violence Begins at Home. A Comprehensive Guide to Understanding and Ending Domestic Abuse.* Alameda, CA: Hunter House.
Women and Law in Southern Africa Research Trust, Botswana (WLSA Botswana). 1992. *Maintenance Laws and Practices in Botswana.* Gaborone: Women and Law in Southern Africa Research Project.
Women and Law in Southern Africa Research Trust, Botswana (WLSA Botswana). 1997. *Botswana Families and Women's Rights in a Changing Environment.* Gaborone: Women and Law in Southern Africa Research Project.
Women and Law in Southern Africa Research Trust, Botswana (WLSA Botswana). 1999. *Chasing the Mirage: Women and the Administration of Justice.* Gaborone: Women and Law in Southern Africa Research Project.
Women and Law in Southern Africa Research Trust, Zimbabwe (WLSA Zimbabwe). 1997. *Continuity and Change. The Family in Zimbabwe.* Harare: WLSA,
Women's Affairs Department. 1998. *Report of the Review of Laws Affecting Women in Botswana.* Gaborone: Women's Affairs Department.
Women's Affairs Division, 1996. *The 4th United Nations World Conference on Women. The Platform for Action: A Summary.* Gaborone: Women's Affairs Division, Women's NGO Coalition, and Department of Non Formal Education

Legislation
Children's Act, 1981 [Cap: 28:04]
Criminal Procedure and Evidence Act [Cap: 08:01]
Constitution of the Republic of Botswana [Cap: 00:1]
Interpretation Act (Section 49)
Marriage Act. [Cap: 29:01]
Penal Code. [Cap: 08:01]
Penal Code (Amendment) Act, 1998 [Cap: 08:01]

Conventions and Declarations
Convention on the Rights of the Child, 1989.
Declaration on the Elimination of Violence Against Women, 1993.
SADC. The Prevention And Eradication of Violence Against Women and Children. An Addendum to the 1997 Declaration on Gender and Development by SADC Heads of State or Government, 1998.

INDEX

Absconding 53–5
Assault 36
Attorney General's Chambers 20, 30, 32–33, 84
Aunt 12, 41

Bail 79
Boy child 3–4, 7
Brother 7, 11, 38, 45
Business community 91–92

Chief(s) *See Traditional leaders*
Child 7–8, 37, 56–57
Child abuse 1, 6, 9, 18, 21, 30, 34–35, 37–38, 40
Children's Act, The 8, 13, 21–22, 84
Children's rights 21–22
Closure, of cases *See Withdrawal of cases*
Cohabitation 47
Common law *See General law*
Consent 7–8, 50, 55, 57, 79
Constitution of Botswana 18
Convention on the Rights of the Child 7–9, 21, 57
Conviction 59, 70
Couselling services 30, 84, lack thereof 70
Criminal Procedure and Evidence Act 18, 53
Culture 3, 7, 14, 31, 33, 35–8, 41
Cultural practices *See Customary laws*
Customary court(s) 3, 25, 40–1, 57
Customary Courts Act 19
Customary law 18–22, 29
Customary practices 19, 36, 37–38, 40, 47, 57–58

Daughter 39, 43– 45, 71
Doctors 25, 27, 36, 74
Doctor(s) reports 25, 27, 36, 74

Economic dependence 4, 35, 39–40. 47, 62
Evidence, insufficient 33, 52–53, 64–65
Evidence gathering 29, 59, 88

Family-based violence 3, 7, 9
Family violence *See Family-based violence*
Father 2, 4, 7, 11, 37, 39, 43–45, 71–72
Female-headed households 47
Form BP 73 *See Medical Form BP 73*
Forensic evidence 53

Gender-based violence *See Gender violence*
Gender training 91
Gender violence 1, 4, 6, 9–12, 14, 17–18, 34
General law 18–22, 29, 57
Girl child 1, 2, 4, 7, 12–13, 34–36, 43, 64
Grandchild 7, 11
Grandfather 7, 12
Grandmother 7, 12

Half siblings 12
Health workers 29
HIV 2, 78
HIV/AIDS testing 82
Human rights 9, 18, 25, 91
Husband 30, 38, 40
Impact of sexual abuse 11
Interpretation Act 7, 81
Investigative diary 75
Investigative skills 51, 53, 88

Justice, administration of 1
Justice delivery system 1, 22

Law, customary *See Customary law*
Law, general *See General law*
Legal education 93
Legal opinion 59, 83
Legal pluralism 14–15, 52

Magistrates 25, 36, 58–59, 67, 78
Magistrate court 25, 32, 40
Magistrate court records 26
Marriage 56, 64, 65–6
Marriage Act 8, 56, 65, 81
Maternal aunt 7, 39, 41
Maternal uncle 4, 7, 37–39, 41, 43, 45–47
Medical evidence 59
Medical examination 50–52, 63, 74
Medical examination form *See Medical Form B.P.73*
Medical form B.P.73 59, 73, 74
Molokomme, A. 14–15, 19
Mother 7, 11, 33, 37–40, 43–44, 70–72

Neighbours 2, 4, 30, 52, 65
Nephew 43
Niece 38, 43
Non-governmental organisations 25, 27, 29–30, 44–45, 68, 70, 72–73, 90–91

Offences against morality 30, 32, 49

Parliament 83, 94
Paternal aunt 1, 39
Paternal uncle 4, 7, 39, 43, 72
Patriarchy 13–14, 16, 35, 38, 45
Penal Code 7, 11, 18, 20, 28, 32, 37, 39–41, 57, 71

Penal Code (Amendment) Act 12, 20, 29, 57
Penalty 36, 40–41
Perpetrator 37–40, 59–61, 66–67
Places of safety 92
Police 13, 25, 27–30, 40, 44, 51, 53–54, 57, 59, 62, 67
Police procedures 29, 53, 73–74, 83
Police records 25–26, 28–32, 49, 60–61, 66–67
Police statement(s) 73
Political will 94
Poverty 2, 16–17, 46–47, 65
Power, abuse of 13–14, 35, 44
Power, imbalance of 9, 11, 13–14, 16, 35, 38, 44
Prosecution 2, 33, 51, 73

Rape 32, 37, 43, 49–52, 54, 57, 66, 74
Roman Dutch law *See General Law*

SADC, Addendum to the 1997 Declaration on Gender and Development 9–10
Safety 4, 61–64
Sexual abuse 3, 9–11, 13–14, 18, 22, 30, 35–36, 40, 43–48, 50, 57, 61–64, 68, 73
Sexually transmitted diseases 2–3, 43, 66, 68–69
Single mothers *See Female-headed households*
Sister 11
Setswana customary practices *See Culture, Customary practices*
Social workers 29, 44, 67, 69
Socialization 8, 11, 35–36, 40, 42, 52, 61, 82
Son 43–44
Stepbrother 12, 39, 47
Stepdaughter 7, 43–45, 47
Stepfather 2, 4, 7, 11–12, 30, 37, 39, 41, 43–

45, 47, 71
Stepmother 7, 12, 39, 41, 47
Stepsister 12, 39, 47
Stepson 7, 47
Students 2, 4–5, 25, 27–28, 36–37, 49, 55–57, 65
Survivor 25, 31

Teenage pregnancies 2–5, 26, 39– 40, 45–46, 49, 58, 60, 67
Traditional leaders 25, 27, 29, 36, 40–42, 48, 57–58, 71
Trial 33, 45

Uncle 2, 4, 12, 39–41, 62, 72
Underreporting, of cases 32, 34–36, 49, 66–67

Victim 34, 43, 59–62, 66–68
Violence against women 1–3, 9–10, 18, 30

Warrant of arrest 63, 73, 79
Withdrawal of cases 33, 39, 51–53, 54, 62, 73
Women's NGO Coalition 90
Women's rights 9, 16

www.ingramcontent.com/pod-product-compliance
Lightning Source LLC
Chambersburg PA
CBHW052131010526
44113CB00034B/1671